Contents

Contents

SNAKES

Learn more about the slithering marvels of nature.

Snakes, Snakes Everywhere

Based on their skeletal structure, snakes have been divided into over 15 families. Of these, the colubrids, elapids, vipers, pit vipers, boas and pythons are well-known.

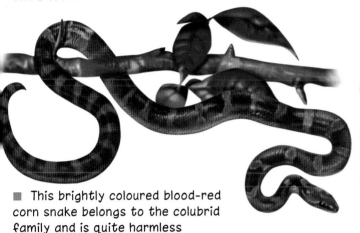

■ This brightly coloured blood-red corn snake belongs to the colubrid family and is quite harmless

Colubrids

Snakes of the Colubridae family are popularly called colubrids. There are around 1,800 species in this category, making it the largest snake family. Colubrids include most of the harmless snakes, such as the rat snake, the common water snake and the grass snake.

Elapids

The Elapidae family comprises over 250 species of snakes, all of which are poisonous. Elapids are commonly referred to as the cobra family. This family includes all cobras, kraits, mambas and coral snakes.

■ Although they resemble vipers, death adders are actually elapids. They are extremely poisonous and are found in almost all parts of Australia

Vipers and pit vipers

Vipers are divided into two main groups – true vipers and pit vipers. The Viperidae family is made up of 50 species of true vipers. A Russell's viper is a kind of true viper. Pit vipers belong to the Crotalinae family. There are around 100 species in this family. They can be distinguished from vipers by the heat-detecting pits between their eyes and nostrils. Rattlesnakes and bushmasters are pit vipers.

Boas and pythons

Anacondas and boas belong to the Boidae family. Of the 70 species, most have large, muscular bodies and kill their prey by coiling around it. The anaconda, a water boa, is considered to be the heaviest snake. Pythons belong to a sub-family of Boidae. They, too, kill their prey by suffocating it.

INTERESTING FACT!

Snakes of the *Boidae* family are believed to be the oldest in the world. They existed even during the age of dinosaurs. The snakes of this family are the only ones that possess two lungs, instead of just one elongated lung!

Know Your Fangs

One of the easiest ways of identifying the different kinds of snakes is by their teeth and fangs. The structure and arrangement of these differ from family to family. Most poisonous snakes have two hollow fangs attached to the upper jaw. Depending on their teeth and fangs, snakes are broadly classified into four groups.

■ Although most rear-fanged snakes are not dangerous to humans, the bite of African boomslangs can prove fatal

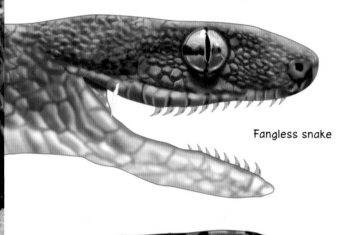

Fangless snake

Fangless snakes

These snakes are called Aglyphs, and they do not have fangs to inject poison. However, they have several large teeth curved inwards. This helps in gripping prey while killing it. Fangless snakes include blind snakes, pythons, boas, and some colubrids.

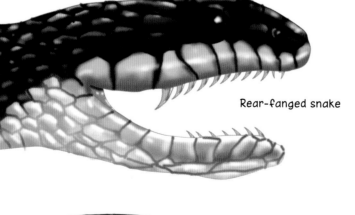

Rear-fanged snake

Rear-fanged snakes

Snakes in this category are known as Opistoglyphs, and they have two to four long fangs. As the name suggests, these fangs are placed towards the back of the snake's mouth. A number of colubrids make up this group.

Front-fanged snake

Front-fanged snakes

Almost all elapids are front-fanged, or Proteroglyphs. Their fangs are fixed. Since they cannot be folded the fangs have to be short – making sure that the snake does not bite itself when it closes its mouth. The cobra is the most famous of front-fanged snakes.

■ The long fangs of pit vipers help them to inject the poison deep into the body of the prey

Fang sheath
Venom gland
Venom duct
Hollow rectractable fangs
Eye
Nostril
Heat sensing pit

Pipe-grooved snakes

All vipers and pit vipers fall under this category. They are called Solenoglyphs. These snakes have long fangs attached to the front of the upper jaw. These fangs can be moved at will, and are kept folded when not in use.

Small curved teeth

Extendable glottis allows breathing while ingesting prey

Forked tongue

INTERESTING FACT!

The Gaboon viper of Africa has the longest fangs. They can grow up to 5 cm (2 inches) in length. Interestingly, the Gaboon viper's venom is not as toxic as some of the other species'.

9

A Scaly Tale

Snakes have a long and cylindrical body and their bone structure and organs are adjusted to this shape. The body of the snake is covered with dry scales. Bigger scales on the belly help in gripping the ground.

The whole length

The slender body of snakes is ideal for slithering and creeping into small holes. Since snakes are long and narrow, paired organs like lungs and kidneys are placed one in front of the other. Most snakes have a single, narrow lung that does the work of two. In some sea snakes, this lung stretches along the entire body to keep the snake afloat.

■ It is easy to identify snakes by studying the unique patterns on their scales. For instance, the Indian cobra has a spectacle-shaped pattern on its hood, which distinguishes it from other snakes in the family

INTERESTING FACT!

Snakes cannot close their eyes! This is because they do not have moveable eyelids. The snake's eyes are protected by a special transparent scale called the brille or spectacle!

■ This African egg-eating snake can swallow eggs even thrice the size of its head whole! This is made possible by its special jaws and the folds of interstitial skin, which provide the snake with its flexibility

Shaped to adapt

Snakes have different body shapes depending on their habitat. Snakes like vipers and cobras have circular bodies with strong muscles. This helps them to get a better grip on sand and rocks. Water snakes and sea snakes have a flattened body with paddle-like tail that helps them to push through water.

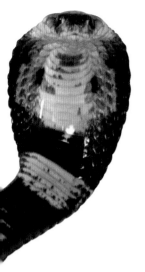

Brand new skin

The outer layer of skin becomes old over time and has to be replaced regularly. This is done by shedding it after a new, healthy layer has developed underneath. This is called moulting. Some snakes moult every 20 days, while others do it only once a year.

■ To remove its old skin, the snake breaks it by rubbing itself against a rock or any other rough surface. It then crawls out of the dead skin, turning it inside out

Scales that tell tales

One can tell where a particular snake lives by looking at its scale. Snake scales can be rough or smooth depend-ing upon the snake's environment. Snakes that live in wetlands, marshes and rivers have keeled (ridged) scales that help the snakes to balance themselves in the wet surroundings. Some water and sea snakes have rough sandpaper-like scales that help them to grip their prey better. Burrowing snakes have smooth scales, which enable them to move through soil easily.

Smooth Skin

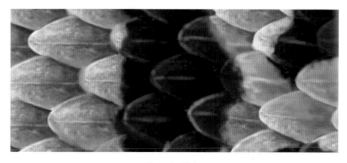
Rough Skin

Sharp Senses

Snakes rely on a number of senses like smell, heat, sight, sound and touch. Some have more refined senses than others. Through millions of years of evolution, snakes have developed senses that are unique in the animal world. Most of these features came about since they live at ground level and do not have legs.

There is a small opening on the upper lip that enables the snake to flick its tongue in and out without having to open its mouth

Sound and touch

Snakes do not have external ears, but they can hear. Ground vibrations are transmitted through the body to a bone that connects the lower jaw and the skull. An inner ear then picks up the vibrations. Snakes are also very responsive to touch. They can feel the slightest change on the ground.

More than a nose

Snakes have a nose, but they possess another advanced sense of smell. Their forked tongue picks up chemical traces and transfers them into pits on the roof of the mouth. These pits, called Jacobson's organ, analyse the chemicals and help the snake to identify its prey.

- Brain
- Nerve
- Jacobson's organ
- Forked tongue
- Eye
- Nostril

California night snake

Turn on the heat

Certain snakes, like the California night snake, are able to sense the heat of other creatures. This is most developed in vipers, pythons and boas. Heat-detecting sensors pick up the difference in temperatures between the prey and the surroundings. Snakes can thus strike even in the dark.

INTERESTING FACT!

Certain animals, such as Siberian chipmunks, smear themselves with snake urine or roll over dead snakes so that they smell like snakes. Studies have revealed that snakes are less likely to attack prey which have a smell like their own!

Whip snake
[day hunter]

Prey spotting

Most snakes have good eyesight, but they get a limited view because they are ground creatures. They are good at detecting movement but weak at identifying colours. The eyes of snakes are also adapted to their surroundings. Tree snakes that catch birds have large pupils, similar to those that hunt at night. Some burrowing snakes like blind snakes have eyes that only distinguish between light and darkness.

Horned viper
[night hunter]

■ Snakes that are active at night usually have small eyes, while those that hunt during the day have large eyes. Some snakes like the vine snake even have 3D vision, since its eyes are located at the front of its head

On the Move

Snakes have developed an efficient way of moving about that more than makes up for their lack of legs. The slithering movement may suggest that they do not have bones. In fact, they actually use their bones, muscles and scales to move. The muscles help the ribs pull the scales forward and backward, which in turn helps in locomotion. Snakes move in four different ways.

■ The brown tree snake uses the concertina movement to climb trees. It first coils its tail around a branch, using the neck to cling on to a higher branch. The snake then pulls up the rest of its body.

Rectilinear movement

Serpentine movement

Concertina movement

Serpentine movement

Most snakes use the serpentine motion, also called lateral undulation. They produce muscular waves by tightening and relaxing a set of muscles. The tail pushes against the surface. The two actions together thrust the snake forward in an 'S' pattern. Some snakes can move at speeds of 10 km/h (6.2 mph) in this fashion.

Concertina

In this movement the snake anchors the front of its body to the surface and pulls up the rest of its body behind. It then uses this part to push the front part forward – quite like a caterpillar. Most snakes use this movement to climb trees and to move through narrow spaces.

Desert snakes, like the sidewinder rattlesnake, use the sidewinding motion. Only small parts of the snake's body touch the hot ground giving the appearance that the snake is jumping

Sidewinding

This is a spectacular movement that snakes use to move on sandy surfaces. They anchor their heads on the ground and push the body sideways after forming an arc. A part of the body travels through the air before touching the sand.

Sidewinder movement

Rectilinear

Large snakes such as boas and pythons move in this manner. They extend the scales under their belly to push against the ground and move in a fairly straight line.

■ Sea snakes and other water snakes use the lateral movement to swim in water. They push their sides against the water and use their paddle-like tails for additional thrust

INTERESTING FACT!

The poisonous yellow-bellied sea snake can swim at more than 3 km/h (1.86 mph). It is the fastest among sea snakes, and lives along the Pacific Coast of North America.

15

Family Tree

Snakes are not very social. They prefer to live and hunt alone. A father snake, a mother snake and their young would indeed make an unusual picture.

■ Baby rattlesnakes are as dangerous as the adults. They have short fangs with venom right from the time they are born

Happy birthday

Snakes have two different ways of giving birth. Most of them lay eggs, from which the babies later hatch. Such snakes are called oviparous. Some do not lay eggs. Instead, the babies hatch inside the mother, who then gives birth to her young. These snakes are ovoviviparous.

Eggsactly!

Snakes' eggs are soft, tough and leathery. The shell is not hard like birds' eggs. The babies take some time to wriggle out of them. The mother lays the eggs in damp and warm spots, and tries to hide them from egg-eating predators.

■ Most birds of prey eat snakes. Eagles and owls are known to feed on both adult snakes and their young ones

Mama's love

Mother snakes are not very caring. They do not stay long with their new-borns. But there are exceptions. The Indian python, for example, is very protective of its eggs. The snake coils its body around the eggs and shivers to keep them warm. King cobras make elaborate nests for their eggs.

Young and brave

Newborn snakes are fiercely independent, and can take care of themselves. In some cases, they can be more venomous than their parents. They also shed their skin more frequently. Since they are small, young snakes are always in danger of being hunted by birds and other snakes. Kingsnakes and cobras feed on smaller snakes.

■ A new-born emerald tree boa is usually red or orange in colour. In the course of one year, the snake slowly turns golden yellow before turning completely green. This phenomenon is known as juvenile polymorphism. The green colour of the adult snake keeps getting darker as it grows older

Attack and Defence

Most snakes are not aggressive by nature. They strike only for food and to defend themselves. Since they do not have legs, snakes have developed unique tactics to hunt and protect themselves.

Strike mode

The most common form of attack is to bite the prey. Snakes like the cobra rise high above the ground while striking. But most snakes, such as vipers and pit vipers, creep up slowly and quietly, and strike swiftly when the prey is within reach. If there is a chance of the prey being dangerous, a snake will bite and release it, waiting for the venom to work.

■ The venom of a cobra, a neurotoxin, affects the nervous system. The venom paralyses the nerves that control the heart and the respiratory system. Cobras are immune to venom produced by their own kind

■ Most poisonous snakes inject their venom into the prey and wait for it to die. But some of them swallow their prey alive. Most tree snakes, like this parrot snake, hold on to the branches with their tail and swallow their prey upside down!

Deadly coils

Snakes like boas and pythons, are not poisonous. They have other ways of killing their prey. These snakes wrap their body around their prey in coils. The coils are slowly tightened until the victim suffocates and dies. Anacondas are sometimes known to drag their prey underwater and drown it.

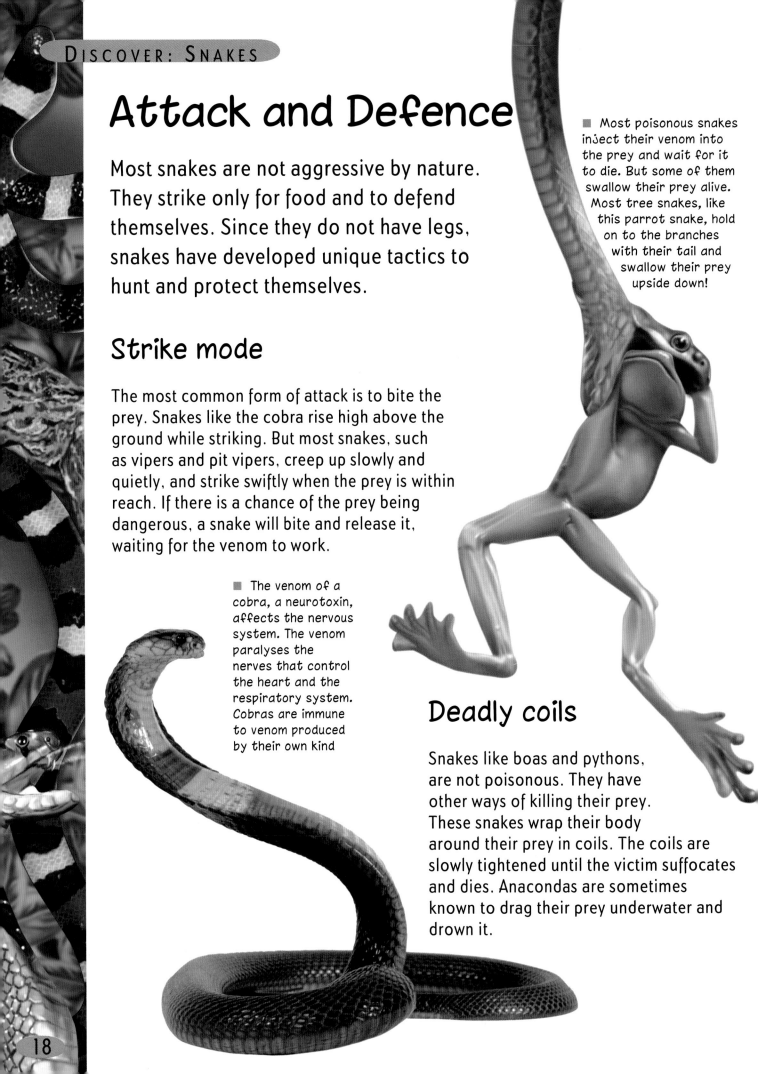

Retreat policy

Snakes are naturally equipped for defence. Camouflages in earth tones make it tough for predators to spot them. For instance, some tree snakes are as green as leaves, and will hide and remain still when they are in danger. Certain snakes, such as the false coral snake, mimic the colour patterns of poisonous snakes to fool attackers. Some cobras have false eye spots on the back of their head to scare predators away. However, most snakes prefer to escape to safety if they are alerted on

FACT FILE

Rattlesnakes shake their tails to warn predators
Hog-nosed snakes turn over and play dead as a defence mechanism
Birds are the biggest enemy of snakes
Snakes swallow their prey whole
Constriction does not crush the prey. It prevents it from breathing and suffocates it

■ Both these snakes are found in Central America. They have the same colour and bands that make them look like identical twins! But upon closer examination one will notice that the false coral snake's tail has red in it, unlike the yellow and black tail of the coral snake

INTERESTING FACT!

The Chinese martial art *t'ai chi* is said to be inspired by the speed and controlled movement of snakes. *T'ai chi* is all about reflexes, flexibility, balance and concentration. It is popular form of relaxation and self-defence.

The rattle of the rattlesnake

Innovations

Snakes have special defence techniques. The most famous, of course, is the rattlesnake, which rattles its scaly tail to make a loud noise. The cobra raises its hood and hisses in warning. Some harmless snakes open their mouth wide to scare their attackers. The hog-nosed snake can even pretend to be dead!

The Cobra

The cobra is famous for its deadly bite and its raised, expandable hood. When disturbed, it flares this hood and creates a scary yet fascinating image. Several varieties of cobras are found throughout Asia and Africa.

King cobra

This is the world's longest venomous snake. It is, on average, 3.6 m (12 feet) long, but is known to grow up to 5.5 m (18 feet). It is olive or brown in colour and often has yellow or white bands. It makes a low hissing sound that sounds more like a dog's growl. The king cobra's hood lacks pattern distinguishing it from other cobras. The king cobra has to rise while attacking because it can only strike downwards. In fact, it can rise up to 1.8 m (6 feet) – that is as tall as a full-grown man!

■ The Egyptian banded cobra, or asp, is found along the northern coast of Africa. Ancient Egyptians believed that this snake could spit fire. Pharaohs used the snake as a protective symbol on their crowns. It is believed that Cleopatra killed herself by making an asp bite her tongue

The king's venom

The venom of the king cobra is not as strong as other cobras. But it is feared because it injects more poison when it bites. It mostly feeds on other snakes, and does not attack humans unless disturbed. Enough of its poison could kill an elephant.

■ The king cobra is the only snake that makes nests for its eggs. The female king cobra uses leaves, twigs and soil to make nests in bamboo groves

Spitting cobra

This snake can spray venom from a distance of about 2.5 m (8 feet) into the eyes of its victims, causing temporary blindness. The black-necked spitting cobra and the Mozambique spitting cobra are well-known.

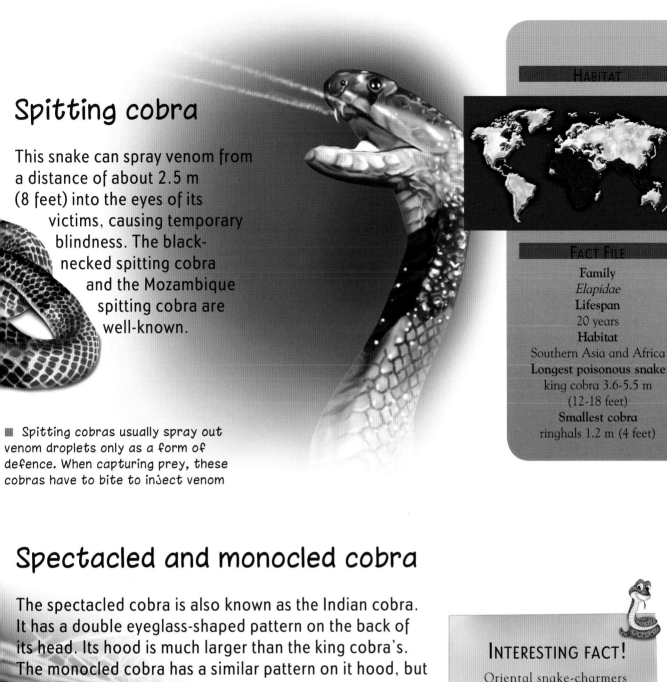

■ Spitting cobras usually spray out venom droplets only as a form of defence. When capturing prey, these cobras have to bite to inject venom

Spectacled and monocled cobra

The spectacled cobra is also known as the Indian cobra. It has a double eyeglass-shaped pattern on the back of its head. Its hood is much larger than the king cobra's. The monocled cobra has a similar pattern on it hood, but with a single (mono) ring.

INTERESTING FACT!

Oriental snake-charmers entertain people by making the snake sway to the music of their flute. But the cobra cannot hear the tune. It actually reacts to the movement of the flute.

Although the spectacled, or Indian, cobra, causes a huge number of human deaths, its venom is used in painkillers and also in the development of anti-venom

Mambas and Kraits

Both mambas and kraits belong to the cobra family. Mambas are long, swift and poisonous snakes found in Africa. They have big eyes. Most of them prefer to stay on trees. Kraits are found only in Asia. They are slender and have a narrow head.

■ During the spring season, male black mambas can be seen fighting. They raise and intertwine their bodies during combat, which is often mistaken for mating

Black mamba

This is the most well-known of all mambas and is feared by humans because of its speed and venom. Despite its name, the black mamba is not actually black in colour. It has a brownish-grey body with a light belly. It gets its name from the purple-black lining in its mouth, which is displayed when the snake feels threatened. The black mamba feeds on small mammals and birds, and spends more time on the ground. Black mambas are normally found in pairs or groups.

Green mamba

The bright green colour of this mamba helps it to hide in trees. It feeds on small birds and lizards. Unlike the black mamba, the green mamba travels alone. The Eastern green mamba is the smallest in the mamba family.

■ Kraits live very close to human habitats. They also show a tendency to hide in shoes, tents and sleeping bags. Most of the attacks involving kraits are accidental due to this particular behaviour

Common krait

This snake is generally slate-coloured with thin white bands. It can grow up to 1.8 m (6 feet). The common krait frequents open grasslands and semi-arid regions. They are also seen in cultivated fields and in wet areas, such as near wells and tanks.

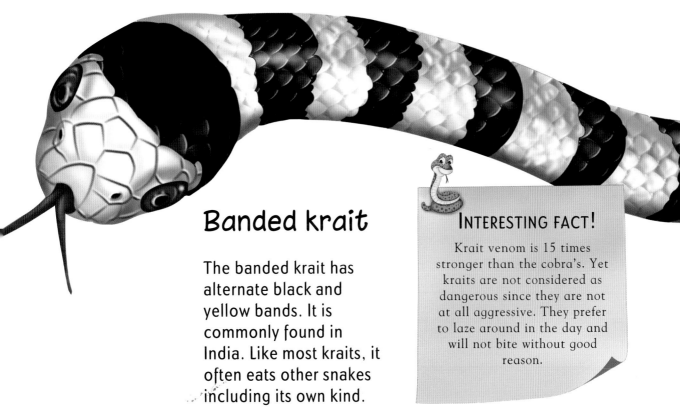

Banded krait

The banded krait has alternate black and yellow bands. It is commonly found in India. Like most kraits, it often eats other snakes including its own kind.

INTERESTING FACT!

Krait venom is 15 times stronger than the cobra's. Yet kraits are not considered as dangerous since they are not at all aggressive. They prefer to laze around in the day and will not bite without good reason.

Coral Snakes and Sea Snakes

Coral snakes are found in Central and South America. They are small but highly venomous and very colourful. Sea snakes are most common in the warm waters of the Indian and Pacific oceans. They are not very long, but can be ten times more venomous than rattlesnakes. Coral snakes and sea snakes also belong to the Elapidae family.

■ Not all coral snakes have colourful bands. In albino coral snakes the bands might be completely absent, or the black bands might be grey or missing. The yellow and red bands could either be normal or very faint

Coiled tales

Coral snakes, with their red, orange, yellow and black bands, are very attractive. But these snakes are seldom seen because they hunt at night. Coral snakes have small and fixed fangs and they bite only when attacked. They have a habit of curling up in tight coils when threatened.

INTERESTING FACT!

Sea snakes can spend long periods underwater because they have a lung that extends almost throughout the length of their body. They can also breathe through their skin.

Sea krait

This is the largest of all sea snakes and is found in most oceans, except the Atlantic. The sea krait is also well-adapted to living on land. It goes ashore to digest its food and shed its skin. The sea krait also returns to land to mate and lay eggs.

■ The yellow-bellied sea snake is the only true sea snake. It never leaves the water to come to the shore. At night, this snake dives to the bottom of the sea and can stay there for almost three hours before coming up to the surface to breathe

■ Coral snakes lay a clutch of 2-13 eggs in the summer. The babies hatch about 60 days later

■ Diamondback water snakes are known to swim through water with their mouths open and swallow as many fish and other smaller creatures as possible

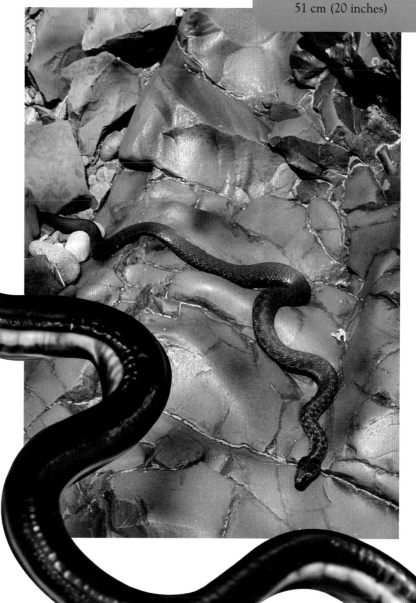

Yellow-bellied sea snake

As its name suggests, this snake has a bright yellow belly. Although it is one of the most poisonous snakes, it attacks only when disturbed. The yellow-bellied sea snake is the fastest of all sea snakes.

25

Vipers

Vipers are highly evolved venomous snakes. They belong to the Viperidae family, and are found in most tropical regions of the world except Australia. They are also known as true, or Old World, vipers. Unlike pit vipers, or New World vipers, they do not have heat-detecting pits.

■ Eyelash pit vipers and the Usambara mountain bush viper look very similar. Both these snakes live on trees and have pointed scales above their eyes that look like eyelashes. Even their colours are similar. However, the Usambara bush viper lacks heat sensors, making it a true viper

Usambara bush viper

Eyelash pit viper

Fearful fangs

Vipers have developed a sophisticated system of survival. They have big, hollow fangs that can be folded into the roof of the mouth when not in use. The venom is delivered through these fangs when the snake bites. The fangs are so sharp and the poison so powerful that often one bite is enough to kill the prey.

Russell's viper

This dangerous snake is abundant in Southeast Asia. Its bite is extremely venomous and is responsible for the most number of human deaths. The Russell's viper is not very long but it is fast and accurate.

FACT FILE

Length of the Russell's viper
1m to 1.5 m (3.3-4.9 feet)
Habitat of the Gaboon viper
dense rainforests of Africa
Weight of the Gaboon viper
16 kg (35.3 pounds)
Distribution of adders
throughout Europe

Gaboon viper

Also called the Gabon viper, its fangs are the longest among all snakes – as big as 5 cm (2 inches)! It is the biggest among Old World vipers, and can grow to almost 2 m (6.6 feet). It is a ground-dwelling snake, and is excellent at camouflaging itself amongst leaves.

INTERESTING FACT!

The viper's venom is harmless as long as it does not enter the blood stream. This has been proven by many courageous people who have conducted experiments by swallowing the poison!

Adder

The best known of this variety is the common adder, or the common European viper. Despite its venom, the adder is not aggressive. It is the only poisonous snake in England, and is less than a metre in length.

■ Most vipers adopt a wait-and-watch approach to capture prey. Some, like this desert horned viper, resort to camouflage tactics. The snake buries itself in the sand, lying still for the prey to come close. Only its head can be seen above the sand

Pit Vipers

Pit vipers are a New World family of poisonous snakes. Like Old World vipers, they too have long fangs. But it is their pits, or heat-detecting organs that make the pit vipers really unique. Most pit vipers are extremely poisonous and can strike when disturbed.

Copperhead

The copperhead is one of the least dangerous venomous snakes in the U.S. It is not very aggressive and has weak venom. Copperheads are very attractive. They are found in several colours, such as brown, pink, orange or yellow. A bright yellow or orange line is found near the mouth.

■ A female bushmaster lays her eggs in burrows built by other animals. Sometimes, the bushmaster even shares the burrow with the particular animal. After laying the eggs, the snake guards them until they hatch. During this period of over 70 days, she does not leave the burrow even to hunt!

Bushmaster

This is the longest poisonous snake in South America. It is believed to be the world's largest pit viper, and can grow to more than 3 m (9.8 feet). Its scales are rough, and it is usually brown or pink in colour. The bushmaster prefers undisturbed tropical forests. The thick foliage provides these snakes with good protection from predators.

Fer-de-lance

This is yet another infamous pit viper from Central and South America. It is known by several names, such as yellow-jaw, yellow tail and barba amarilla. Its venom is believed to have caused more human deaths than any other American snake. It mainly lives on the ground, but also occasionally climbs trees and swims. Fer-de-lances have dark arrowhead markings on their body and can blend into their surroundings very well.

Bad-tempered pit vipers

Some pit vipers are very aggressive. The mangrove, or shore pit viper, the eyelash pit viper and the Habu pit viper may strike without warning. They have very strong venom, which can be fatal.

■ The heat-detecting pits of pit vipers are located between the eyes and nostrils

Pit

INTERESTING FACT!

A snake's venom helps it to digest its food faster. The more the venom the faster the digestion. It has been found that without its venom a fer-de-lance would take twice the time to digest its meal.

■ Cottonmouth, commonly known as water moccasin, gets its name from the white colour inside its mouth. If threatened this snake often opens its mouth to display this feature

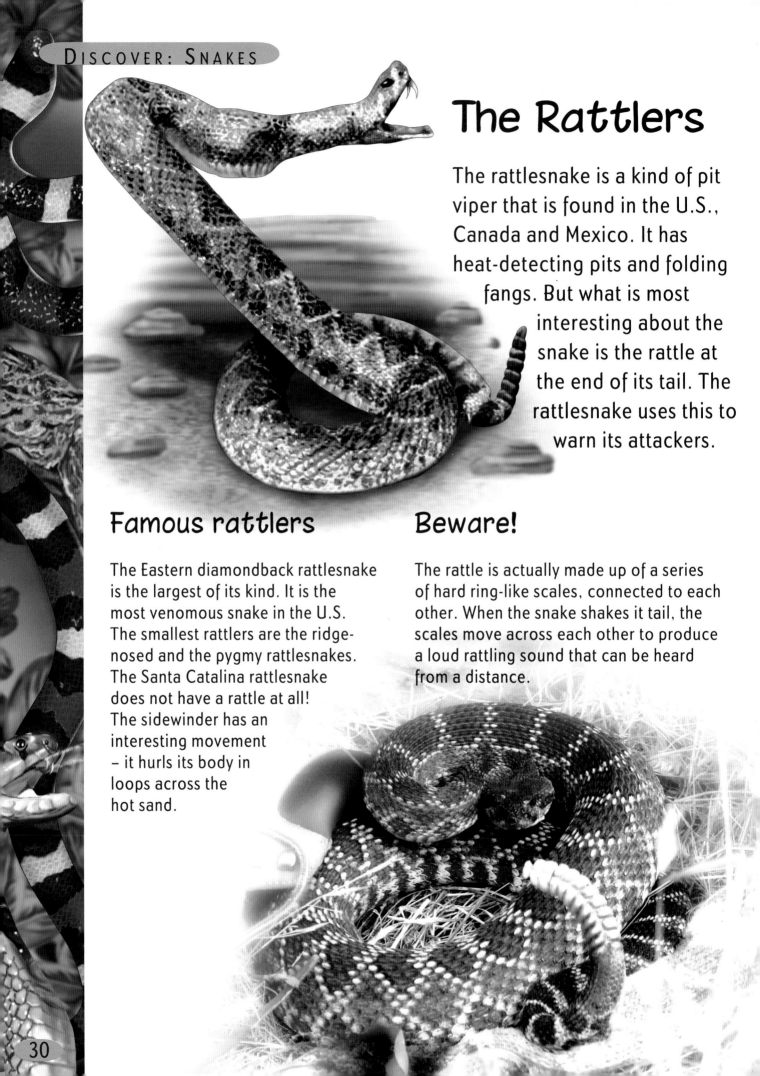

The Rattlers

The rattlesnake is a kind of pit viper that is found in the U.S., Canada and Mexico. It has heat-detecting pits and folding fangs. But what is most interesting about the snake is the rattle at the end of its tail. The rattlesnake uses this to warn its attackers.

Famous rattlers

The Eastern diamondback rattlesnake is the largest of its kind. It is the most venomous snake in the U.S. The smallest rattlers are the ridge-nosed and the pygmy rattlesnakes. The Santa Catalina rattlesnake does not have a rattle at all! The sidewinder has an interesting movement – it hurls its body in loops across the hot sand.

Beware!

The rattle is actually made up of a series of hard ring-like scales, connected to each other. When the snake shakes it tail, the scales move across each other to produce a loud rattling sound that can be heard from a distance.

Rattlesnakes usually
live and hunt alone
But in winters
they hibernate in huge
numbers
Varieties
there are 16 different
varieties of rattlesnakes
Litter size
9 to 10 babies
**Length of the Eastern
diamondback rattlesnake**
1.4-2.4 m (4.6-7.9 feet)

■ Strangely, the rattlesnake does not use its rattle when it comes across a kingsnake. Instead, it raises the front part of its body to appear bigger. But the kingsnake (in the picture on the left) is not frightened by this behaviour and swallows the rattler!

Rattle tale

A rattlesnake is not born with a rattle. A newborn rattler only has a 'button' at the tip of its tail. Every time it sheds its skin, a ring is added to form the rattle. Sometimes a ring or a part of the rattle may fall off due to friction.

The young and the venomous

The rattlesnake is ovoviviparous. The mother does not lay eggs in a nest. Instead, the eggs remain inside her body until they hatch. Baby rattlers can take care of themselves as soon as they're born. In some cases, they are more venomous than their parents.

■ Unlike other rattlesnakes, which prefer deserts or other arid regions, the timber rattlesnake is found in thick forests

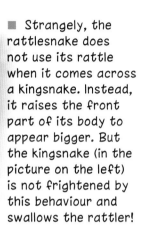

INTERESTING FACT!

Rattlesnakes thrust their way in water as they do on ground. They are excellent swimmers, and some of them may be spotted miles out into the sea. Most rattlesnakes hold their rattles above water to keep them dry!

The Python

Not all snakes are poisonous. Pythons and boas are non-venomous. But they are big, strong and muscular. These snakes kill their prey by constricting, or squeezing it in their coils, until the prey suffocates.

Reticulated python

This is the longest of all snakes. It averages 5-8 m (16.4-26.2 feet), but can grow up to 10 m (32.9 feet)! It is found near the rivers and ponds of Southeast Asian jungles. The reticulated python is an excellent swimmer and tree climber. It is a nocturnal snake.

The rock python

The African and Indian rock pythons are famous for the beautiful patterns on their skin. They live among rocks and on trees. The Burmese rock python is a well-known sub-group of the Indian variety.

■ Some pythons exhibit a condition called albinism. An albino python might lack or not have enough melanin, the pigment that gives the snake its natural colour. Albino pythons could be white, yellow, orange or brown. Most albinos have red eyes and tongues

Green tree python

Compared to others in its family, the green tree python is slimmer and smaller. It largely lives on trees and rarely climbs down. The bright green body of the snake helps it to hide among leaves and surprise its prey. It is hard to distinguish the green tree from the South American emerald tree boa. Both these snakes are very similar in colour and habits.

■ Like all snakes, the python can stretch its jaws wide. But since the python has to hold on to its prey while killing it, their jaws are more rigid than those of the other snakes

Longest python reticulated python: a specimen that was shot in Indonesia in 1912 measured 10 m (32 feet 9.5 inches)
Length of the rock python 5.5-6 m (18-20 feet)
Length of the royal python 1-1.5 m (3-6 feet)
Litter size of pythons 75 babies

INTERESTING FACT!

The giant African python that roamed the earth about 55 million years ago is considered to be the biggest snake that ever lived. It is believed that the snake was about 11.8 m (38.7 feet) long!

The royal and blood pythons

The royal python is found in Africa, and is one of the smaller pythons. It is also known as the ball python because of its ability to coil itself tightly into a ball when in danger. The blood python has irregular blood-red patterns on its skin. It is found in Southeast Asia. Its colouration helps it hide among branches and dead leaves.

■ Pythons are known to swallow animals as large as caimans and monkeys

Boas

Like pythons, boas too suffocate their prey before swallowing it whole. However, unlike pythons, boas hatch their eggs inside their body. They are the subject of many a horror jungle tale. Explorers have spun stories of having seen monster boas. In reality, they are shorter than pythons but much heavier.

■ Green anacondas are the world's heaviest snake. Growing up to 9 m (29.5 feet) in length an adult green anaconda can be as heavy as 250 kg (551 pounds)

Common boa constrictor

This famous boa constrictor grows up to 3.5 m (11.5 feet) and is found in Central and South American jungles. Like all boas, it has powerful muscles and suffocates its prey. Bats are its favourite meal.

Anaconda

This is one of the most powerful predators in the animal kingdom and it can grow over 9 m (29.5 feet). It prefers still waters and marshy areas. Hence, it is also known as the water boa. Its eyes and nostrils are at the top of its head. This helps it move in the water without being seen. The anaconda's prey can be as large as pigs and deer.

Amazon tree boa

The Amazon tree boa is found in South American tropical forests. Its large pupils help this snake to hunt at night, while its slim body aids the boa to move swiftly on trees. It has a long striking range. It can hang from a branch and squeeze its prey in the air!

■ The anaconda's teeth are curved backwards making it impossible for the prey to escape the powerful jaws once caught

HABITAT

FACT FILE

Lifespan of boas
20-30 years
Number of young ones
20-60 born alive
Anaconda length
6.1-9.1 m (20-30 feet)
Boa constrictor average length
4 m (13 feet)

Other boas

The emerald tree boa is another tree-dwelling boa. The patterns on its skin help the snake to hide among the branches. The spotted sand boa hides in the sand and pounces on the unsuspecting prey.

■ When sunlight falls on the scales of a rainbow boa, the skin appears blue, green and violet, giving the snake its name

BIG CATS

A Cat's World

Did you know that the common house cat is related to the lions and tigers that you may have seen at the zoo? They are members of the same family called Felidae. Each family is special and the curious world of cats is no different.

■ The whole world is made up of what are called ecosystems, where living beings live interdependently and feed on one another. The big cats feed on smaller animals like deer, which in turn eat grass and leaves. Such a cycle is called a food chain

Body structure

Most cats have similar skeletons. They have rounded heads and their body structure allows them to move swiftly and silently. Their backbone is very different from humans. While ours is very rigid, the cat's flexible spine allows it to bend into a ball!

Meat lovers

Cats are hunters and love meat. Domestic cats hunt for mice, while lions, tigers and jaguars hunt in the wild. They prey on other wild animals for food.

Living den

Big cats are native to all continents except Australia and Antarctica. But most of the 36 species of wild cats are in danger. Many scientists believe that many of them may not be around within the next 25 years.

■ Big cats have special hunting skills. Most like to stalk their prey before attacking

The king of the jungle is among the mightiest of all big cats

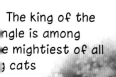

On the prowl

They have large eyes, excellent hearing, sharp teeth and strong limbs with sharp claws. This makes them good hunters. Most have long tails and their fur is usually spotted or striped.

INTERESTING FACT!

Cats have more bones than humans. Humans have only 206 bones in their body, whereas the cat has 230. About 10 per cent of a cat's bones are in its tail. The tail is used to maintain balance.

37

Cat Family

Cats in the wild are classified as small, medium and large depending on their size. They are also divided into three groups based on their traits. These are Felinae, Pantherinae and Acinonychinae.

Domestic vs wild

Domestic cats and their wild relatives share many characteristics. They have short, strong jaws and sharp teeth. All cats are good hunters. But while smaller cats like to eat standing, big cats like to lie down and eat their food.

■ Domestic cats hold their tails low and swing them to indicate that they are feeling playful or nervous. An upright tail is usually a sign of alertness. Big cats behave similarly

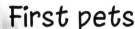

■ The polecat has a long, slender body and short legs. It feeds on rats, mice, rabbits, fish, eggs and fruit but, despite its misleading name, is not a member of the cat family

First pets

Archaeological studies show that human beings have kept pet cats for nearly 8,000 years. In Egypt, 4,000 years ago, they were kept because of their skill to hunt snakes, rats and mice. The Egyptians also worshipped cats and believed they were forms of the Goddess Bast. It was a crime to kill cats or trade in them.

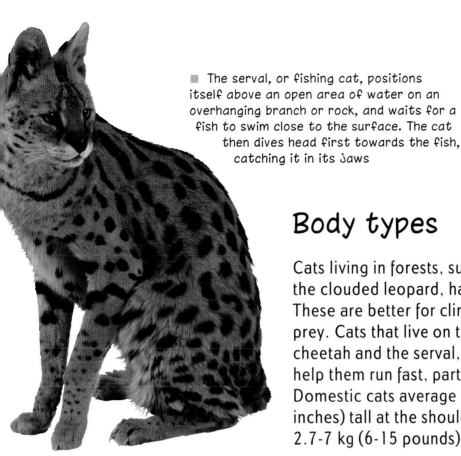

■ The serval, or fishing cat, positions itself above an open area of water on an overhanging branch or rock, and waits for a fish to swim close to the surface. The cat then dives head first towards the fish, catching it in its jaws

Body types

Cats living in forests, such as the jaguar and the clouded leopard, have short, stocky limbs. These are better for climbing trees and ambushing prey. Cats that live on the savannah, such as the cheetah and the serval, have long limbs. These help them run fast, particularly when chasing prey. Domestic cats average about 20-25 cm (8-10 inches) tall at the shoulder and weigh from 2.7-7 kg (6-15 pounds).

Purr and meow

Some scientists say a domestic cat can make more than 60 different sounds and they may have different meanings. For example, a meow can be a friendly greeting, or it may express curiosity, hunger, or loneliness. Purring usually means contentment, but some cats also purr when they are sick. Hisses, growls, and screams indicate anger and fear.

INTERESTING FACT!

Despite its name, the polecat is actually a member of the weasel family and is related to the skunk and the ferret. Similarly, the Australian tiger cat is a marsupial that is closely related to the possum and the Tasmanian Devil.

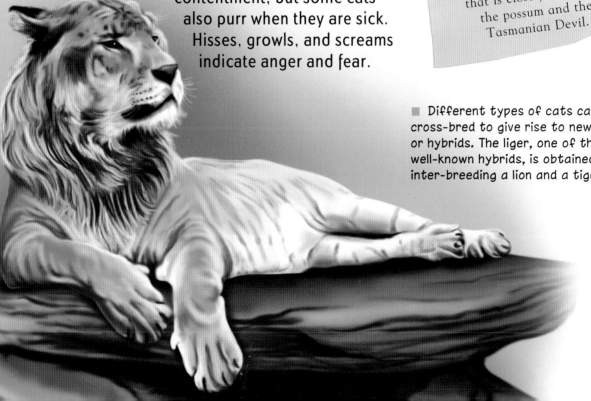

■ Different types of cats can be cross-bred to give rise to new breeds, or hybrids. The liger, one of the most well-known hybrids, is obtained by inter-breeding a lion and a tiger

Cat Senses

These specialist hunters rely on their senses of sight and hearing to locate their prey. They also produce a wide range of sounds, including snarls, growls, purrs and roars. While lions and tigers roar, cheetahs and pumas are tend to purr.

Looking afar

Big cats have excellent day and night vision. Their eyes face forward, allowing both eyes to focus on the same object. Their sharp eyesight allows them to judge distances and the size of the object as well.

■ Apart from its strong muscles and teeth, a tiger also relies on its senses for a successful hunt

Vision at night

The big cat's eye is larger than a human's. A cat has a larger pupil, which allows more light to enter the eye at night. While a human pupil is always circular, the cat can shrink its pupil from a circle into a slit like opening. It does so in bright sunlight, allowing less light to enter the eye.

INTERESTING FACT!

No one knows exactly how a cat sees colour, but they definitely do not see it the way we do. According to most scientists, reds appear darker, while greens appear much more lighter and duller to a cat.

A pair of glowing eyes can look scary at night.

Moving ears

Cats have very sharp hearing and can pinpoint the location of a sound almost immediately. The ear has nearly 20 muscles attached to it. The moment a cat hears a sound, it can move its ears in that direction.

Pinnae

■ The external ears of cats are shaped like a cup and are called pinnae.

■ Cats like tigers can smell the presence of another cat that has left its scent in a marked area

Marked territory

All cats have marked areas, or territories, where they live and will protect them fiercely from other cats. Territories usually include hunting grounds, dens, water spots and resting spots. Big cats mark these territories to warn other cats. They leave their scent by spraying urine in special locations or by scratching on trees. They can also leave their scent by rubbing their chins, cheeks, and tails onto objects.

Of Fur and Claws

Big cats are covered with fur. The fur coat protects the animal in very cold or hot weather. But, more importantly, the unique pattern on it acts as camouflage. Camouflage is the ability of an animal to blend with its surroundings. This makes them nearly invisible!

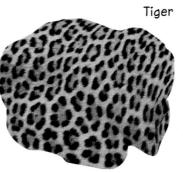

Tiger

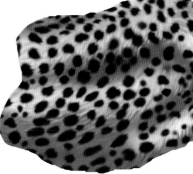

Leopard

Cheetah

■ Cats have different patterns on their coats depending on the habitat in which they live

Protective coat

Just as you wear woollen jumpers in the winter, big cats living in cold areas have thick fur to protect them from the cold. The snow leopard has long, woolly fur which is longer on the animal's belly. This gives extra protection to the part of the body closest to the snow-covered ground. Cats living in warmer climates have short, bristly fur.

■ The small front teeth of the cat mainly function as grooming aids

Invisible coat

A cat's coat is similar to its surroundings. The base colour of the fur is similar to that of the habitat. The lion's yellow/brown fur matches the colouring of the savannah grasslands while stripes on the tiger's coat make it difficult to spot among the tall grasses. The spotted coat of the leopard mimics the patchy sunlight of the forest. Cubs often have spots that fade out as they grow.

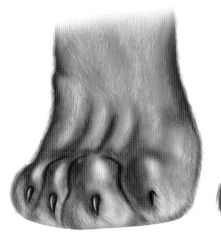
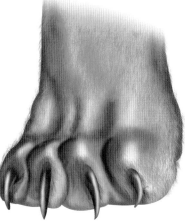

■ With the exception of the cheetah, all cats have retractable claws. These claws are inside the paws, and come out only during combat

Death grip

Claws are a very important hunting tool for cats. With the exception of the cheetah, all cat claws stay covered in their paws. This keeps them safe and sharp. Their claws help the big cats to climb trees, and are also handy while attacking a prey or defending themselves.

INTERESTING FACT!

Long fur is not just to protect against the cold. The black-footed cat and sand cat both have longer fur covering their feet and pads. Both these cats live in desert areas, and the fur protects against the heat of the ground.

Vanity fare

The tongue of the wild cat is much rougher than that of the domestic cat. Its surface is covered with tiny hooks that helps the cat to clean and comb its fur. It also helps them to strip flesh off the bones of their prey.

■ An adult mountain lion may be either grey or reddish-yellow in colour. It does not have any spots

Attack

The cat's body is perfectly built for hunting and killing. It has strong grasping limbs, sharp claws, and knife-like canine teeth. Most cats hunt at dawn or dusk and have excellent senses of vision and hearing. They often have patterned coats that help hide them from their prey.

The stripes on a tiger's body allows it to hide in the grass from its prey

Run and pounce

When the cat senses the right moment, it transfers its bodyweight to its rear legs and lunges towards the victim. This begins the chase. If the cat gets close enough, the prey's run is short. The final phase is the pounce. The cat grabs the animal, and pulls it to the ground. Then it suffocates its prey with its mouth and kills it.

Stalk and ambush

Stalking is when the cat follows its prey silently before attacking. A hunting technique used when a cat hides and attacks suddenly is called an ambush. If an unsuspecting animal comes within striking distance, the cat comes out of hiding and lunges toward its surprised and unprepared victim.

The Lioness is the main hunter in a group, although she is helped by her bigger cubs. The lion only joins in when the prey is big

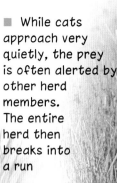

■ While cats approach very quietly, the prey is often alerted by other herd members. The entire herd then breaks into a run

Final kill

Not all cats kill their prey in the same way. Small cats kill their prey with a bite to the back of the neck. Large cats suffocate their prey, either with a stranglehold on the neck or by covering the prey's snout with their jaws.

Success rate

The cheetah is the best hunter within the wild cat species. It catches up to 60-70 per cent of prey that it hunts. The lion on the other hand has a low success rate at less than 30 per cent.

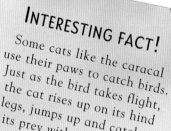

INTERESTING FACT!
Some cats like the caracal use their paws to catch birds. Just as the bird takes flight, the cat rises up on its hind legs, jumps up and catches its prey with an extended paw. Having caught the bird in both paws, it brings it down and eats it.

■ Among the cheetah's hunting skills the final chase down is its most effective weapon. A combination of physical features allow the cheetah to run faster than any other land animal

Defence

While big cats are known to be the most deadly predators, many have had to develop methods to protect themselves from injury during a hunt. They also face threats from other cats who may take over their territory or try and steal their kill from them. Protecting the cubs is the responsibility of the female.

■ A leopard will climb a tree to protect its kill from other animals like lions and hyenas who have been known to steal their prey from them

In the family

A lioness will protect her cubs from other animals and also from lions who pose a threat to them. When a new male lion takes over a pride, he usually kills all the cubs and mates with the lionesses to start his own family. The male lion protects the entire family and his mane makes him look larger to other lions.

Group attack

Lions usually hunt together to increase their chances of killing prey and protecting themselves. They fan out in a semicircle to creep up on the prey. Lions have been known to be injured while hunting larger prey, like giraffes and elephants.

■ A lioness defends the young ones in the pride. It will attack any wild animal that could harm her babies

Defending territory

Big cats like tigers are very protective of
their territory. One male's territory generally
includes three to four females. Males will
aggressively fight each other to defend their
territory. However, neighbouring females have
been known to share their kill.

Animal attack

Other animals also have methods of defending
themselves against the mighty cats. Elephants
kick, rampage, trample and usually succeed in
running away. Zebras snort loudly to alert the
herd of impending danger. The males will position
themselves between the predator and the herd
and kick and bite giving the herd time to escape.
Animals like the wildebeest are known to break
into a stampede.

INTERESTING FACT!

Some cats attack in groups.
A few cats act as 'beaters',
moving openly toward an
intended victim and driving
it in the direction of another
cat lying in wait, ready to
pounce. This strategy is used
by both lynx and lion.

■ When a herd of elephants face
danger, the adults form a circle
around the calves to protect them.
Big cats, however, rarely attacks
elephants because of their sheer
size

47

King of the Savannahs

The lion is often called the king of beasts because it is so big and powerful and because it has no natural predators. The male lion has a mane around its neck that adds to its royal look. Its loud roar is fierce and frightening. Lions are truly majestic and exhibit dominant behaviour.

Living in the open

Unlike tigers, lions don't like living in thick forests. They prefer to roam through open lands, and are usually found in woodlands, grassy plains, and areas with thorny scrub trees. Lions live where they find a steady supply of food, like deer, antelope, zebra and other hoofed animals. Lions also need to live near water.

In zoos and in the wild

Lions are found in eastern and southern Africa. A few hundred can be found in the Gir Forest of India. They are called Asiatic lions. Most lions live in national parks and areas called reserves, where the animals are protected from hunters. Hundreds of lions also live in zoos and are extremely popular performers in circuses.

■ Lion cubs can be tamed easily. Circuses start training lions when they are about two years old

Lion´s mane

Lions are better known for their strength, rather than speed. Male lions are the only cats with manes. This collar of long, thick hair covers the head and the neck down to the shoulders and chest. The mane makes the male look bigger and stronger.

FACT FILE

Average weight about 160-180 kg (353-397 pounds). A large male can weigh up to 230 kg (507 pounds)
Length about 3 m (10 feet)
Height about 1 m (3.2 feet) tall at the shoulder
Lioness weight about 110-140 kg (243-309 pounds)
Lioness height about 30 cm (1 foot) shorter than lions

INTERESTING FACT!

The lion's mane protects him during fights. The long, thick hair softens the enemy's blows. One-year-old cubs have little hair around their heads. The mane is not fully grown until the animal is about 5 years old.

■ Unlike most wild cats, who prefer to live alone, lions love living in one big family, called a pride

The cover of colour

The lion's coat is ideal camouflage while hunting. It is a brownish yellow – the same colour as dead grass. Only the back of the ears and the tuft of hair at the end of the tail are black. Cubs have spots on their coats.

■ The male lions in the pride ordinarily let the lionesses do the hunting for the family. But they kill for themselves when they find prey

The Tiger Trail

The tiger is the largest member of the cat family. After the lion, tigers are perhaps the most awesome of all the big cats. In the old days, kings would hunt tigers for their beautiful fur. The large scale killing of tigers and clearing of forests have left just a few thousands of them in the wild today. Tigers live in the forests of Asia and are part of many a myth and story!

■ Tigers are extremely fast when running short distances and can leap nearly 9 m (30 feet). But if a tiger fails to catch its prey quickly, it will give up the moment it feels tired

Striped giants

Tigers can be easily recognised because of their striped fur and skin. They usually have an orange or brownish yellow coat with a white chest and belly. Their coat is covered with broken vertical black/dark brown stripes. These stripes allow the animal to blend in while walking through tall grass.

Living in shadows

Tigers live in oak wood forests, tall grasslands, swamps and marshes. They are found in the hot rainforests of Malaya, the dry thorn woods of India and the cold, snowy spruce forests of northern China. Tigers rarely go into open spaces like lions do.

■ A tiger marks its territory with urine, claw marks, or by rubbing its tail against a tree or a rock. The scent and mark let other tigers know that the territory is occupied

On the prowl

The tiger usually hunts at night, following animal trails along stream beds. A tiger uses its sharp eyes and keen ears for a hunt, along with its sense of smell. The tiger waits in cover, before rushing its prey and pouncing. Using its sharp claws, the tiger grasps its victim by the side and pulls it to the ground.

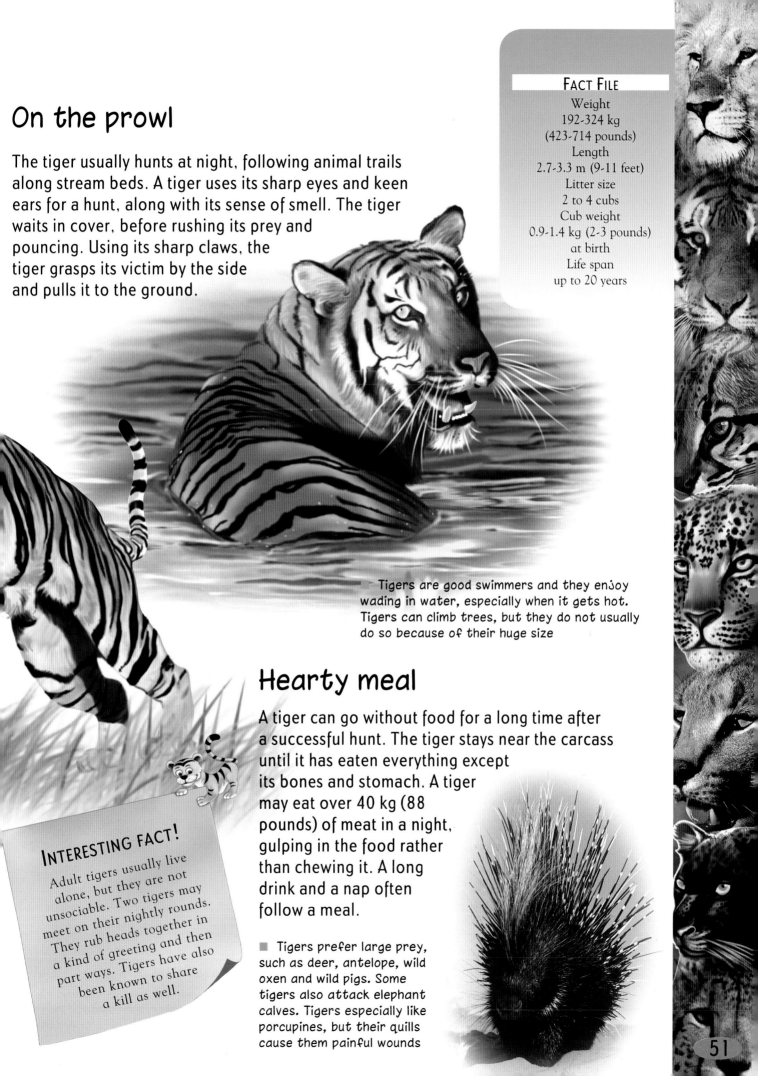

FACT FILE
Weight
192-324 kg
(423-714 pounds)
Length
2.7-3.3 m (9-11 feet)
Litter size
2 to 4 cubs
Cub weight
0.9-1.4 kg (2-3 pounds)
at birth
Life span
up to 20 years

Tigers are good swimmers and they enjoy wading in water, especially when it gets hot. Tigers can climb trees, but they do not usually do so because of their huge size

Hearty meal

A tiger can go without food for a long time after a successful hunt. The tiger stays near the carcass until it has eaten everything except its bones and stomach. A tiger may eat over 40 kg (88 pounds) of meat in a night, gulping in the food rather than chewing it. A long drink and a nap often follow a meal.

INTERESTING FACT!
Adult tigers usually live alone, but they are not unsociable. Two tigers may meet on their nightly rounds. They rub heads together in a kind of greeting and then part ways. Tigers have also been known to share a kill as well.

■ Tigers prefer large prey, such as deer, antelope, wild oxen and wild pigs. Some tigers also attack elephant calves. Tigers especially like porcupines, but their quills cause them painful wounds

51

Tigers in Danger!

There are eight sub-species of tiger. These are the Bali tiger, Bengal tiger, Caspian tiger, Indo-Chinese tiger, Javan tiger, Siberian tiger, South China tiger, and Sumatran tiger. Of these, the Bali tiger, Caspian tiger and Javan tiger are now extinct. The remaining five are also in danger of becoming extinct.

One family

The Indo-Chinese tiger is found in Thailand, south China, Myanmar, Cambodia, Vietnam and parts of Malaysia. These tigers are one of the smaller sub-species. The Siberian tiger is found in Russia and is the largest of all tiger species. The Sumatran tiger is only found on the Indonesian island of Sumatra. It is the smallest of all the tiger species. The South Chinese tiger is considered to be the evolutionary ancestor of all the other tiger sub-species. This tiger is the world's most endangered species.

■ The tigers of Siberia, where the winters are bitterly cold, have long, shaggy, winter coats

Just a few

There are fewer than 200 Siberian tigers in the wild and they are found mainly in Russia. The South China tiger is even rarer. Demand for tiger parts like the eyes, bones and skin for use in traditional Chinese medicine led to an increase in poaching after the 1980s. This has threatened the tiger with extinction.

Man eaters?

There are many tales about Great Bengal Tigers being ferocious man-eaters. Yet almost all wild tigers avoid people. Fatal attacks by tigers on humans are, thankfully, rare. Most tigers would only attack a human if disturbed, or were provoked or injured.

HABITAT

FACT FILE

Numbers in the wild
Great Bengal Tiger
3,030-4,735
Siberian Tiger
160-230
South China Tiger
20-50
Sumatran Tiger
400-500
Indo-Chinese Tiger
1,180-1,790

■ In the Sunderban Reserve, along the coast of the Bay of Bengal in India, tigers are reported to have attacked people. Since tigers are thought to attack only from the rear, the people here wear masks on the backs of their heads. This second "face" is thought to confuse the tigers and thus protect the wearer

INTERESTING FACT!

Many adult males claim a territory as their own and keep other males out. The territory may average about 52 sq km (20 square miles) and usually includes a body of water. Tigers also communicate by using different sounds.

White Bengal tigers

Some tigers have chalk-white fur with chocolate-brown or black stripes. These tigers are called white tigers and they have blue eyes. All other tigers have yellow eyes. White tigers are very rare in the wild. More than 100 white tigers live in the world's zoos.

■ White tigers are a variant of Bengal tigers and are rarely found in the wild anymore. A normal-coloured female can give birth to a litter in which some of the cubs are white

Leopards

Leopards are the third largest big cats, after tigers and lions. They are excellent climbers and, unlike most other wild cats, love living in trees. These cats can in live in various kinds of habitat and also have a wide range of prey. They live in the Saharan regions of Africa, and many Asian countries like Turkey, Korea, Java and India.

◻ Leopards spend most of their lives on tree tops

Clear markings

The leopard is most easily recognised by its rosette patterned coat and extremely long, tail which is darker than the rest of its body. The base colour of the coat varies according to the leopard's habitat. Leopards living in open grasslands are golden yellow, while those found in deserts are yellow or cream in colour. Leopards living in mountain regions are deep gold in colour.

Night hunter

Leopards usually hunt at night, though females with cubs prefer to hunt during the day. These cats hunt all kinds of prey, be it impalas, gazelles, hares, reptiles, small monkeys, or various rodents such as rats, squirrels and porcupines.

Clouded leopards have cloud-like spots on their skin. Found in south eastern Asia, they often hang upside down from tree branches!

■ Snow leopards, found in the snow capped mountains of Russia, China and the Himalayas, have woolly furs. Interestingly, their voice is weak and they cannot roar like other big cats

Strong and mean

Leopards have very strong muscles and can drag a fully grown male antelope or even a young giraffe – weighing up to three times their own body weight – high into the tree tops. Leopards are also known to attack humans and their livestock and can be more dangerous than tigers or lions.

Killed for fur

But humans have also been a threat to these cats. They have killed leopards for their fur. As a result leopards have become rare in many places. Many countries have banned trade in leopard skins to protect the animal.

INTERESTING FACT!

All black leopards - sometimes called black Panthers - are found in the dense, wet forested areas of India and Southeast Asia. Their dark colour gives them an advantage while hunting.

■ Vervet monkeys make a loud barking call when a leopard is near to alert the rest of their group

The Swiftest

The fastest animal on earth, the cheetah is unique in many ways. It looks like a large muscular greyhound, with a sleek body and long, thin but powerful legs. This gives the big cat great speed while on the chase. A fully-grown cheetah can reach speeds greater than 113 km/h (70 mph) – that's the National speed limit in the UK!

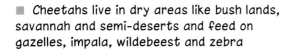

■ Cheetahs live in dry areas like bush lands, savannah and semi-deserts and feed on gazelles, impala, wildebeest and zebra

Following prey

The cheetah hunts mainly by day. It first follows a large herd of gazelle, impala or antelope from a distance. It then selects old, injured or young animals as its prey. The cheetah then chases the animal. The cheetah usually catches its prey in the first attempt.

The kill

The cheetah's powerful jaw muscles enable the cat to grip its prey for several minutes and suffocate the animal by clamping the windpipe. The cheetah has enlarged nasal passages, which enables it to breathe more easily while on the run.

■ Once the kill has been made the cheetah rests to regain its breath. At this time it is vulnerable to hyenas snatching its kill

■ The cheetah's paws are like a dog's. They are narrow and hard padded and non-retractable, unlike other big cats. This allows better grip while running

HABITAT

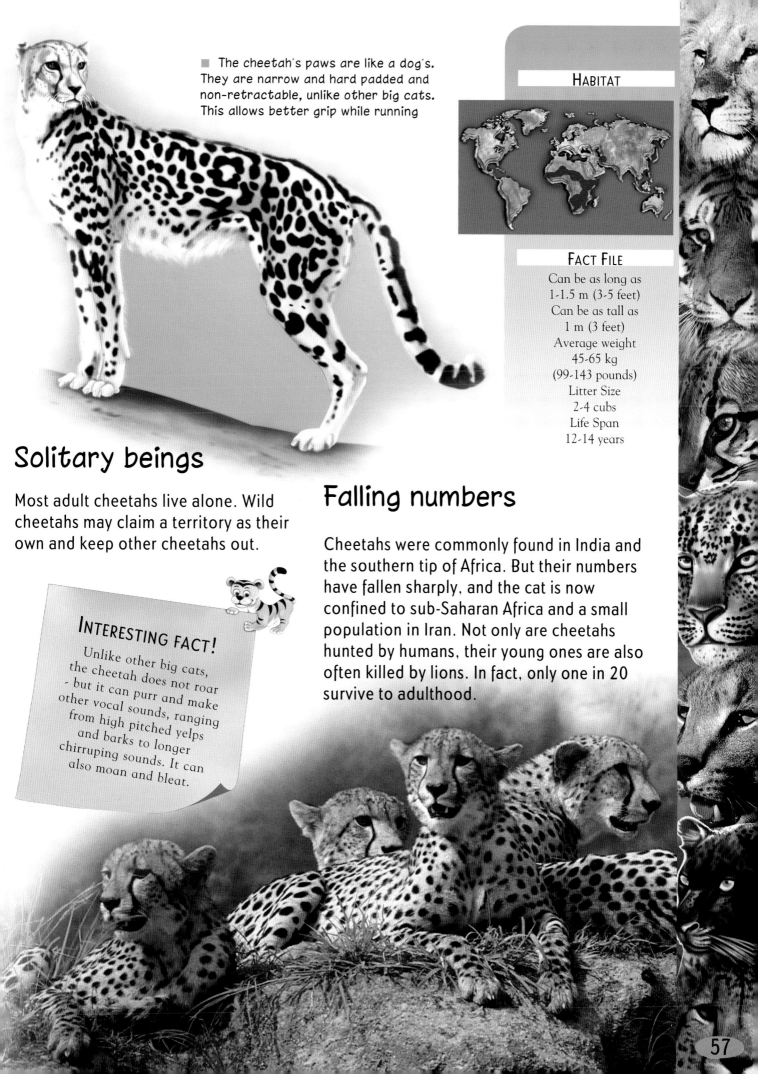

FACT FILE

Can be as long as
1-1.5 m (3-5 feet)
Can be as tall as
1 m (3 feet)
Average weight
45-65 kg
(99-143 pounds)
Litter Size
2-4 cubs
Life Span
12-14 years

Solitary beings

Most adult cheetahs live alone. Wild cheetahs may claim a territory as their own and keep other cheetahs out.

INTERESTING FACT!

Unlike other big cats, the cheetah does not roar - but it can purr and make other vocal sounds, ranging from high pitched yelps and barks to longer chirruping sounds. It can also moan and bleat.

Falling numbers

Cheetahs were commonly found in India and the southern tip of Africa. But their numbers have fallen sharply, and the cat is now confined to sub-Saharan Africa and a small population in Iran. Not only are cheetahs hunted by humans, their young ones are also often killed by lions. In fact, only one in 20 survive to adulthood.

Jaguars of America

Jaguars are often confused with leopards. Both have a similar brownish/yellow base fur colour, with dark rosette markings. But jaguars can be spotted because of the small dots or irregular shapes within the larger rosette markings. They are more stocky and muscular and have a shorter tail.

Living zone

The jaguar is the biggest cat found in the Americas. Jaguars once inhabited areas between the southern states of the U.S. down to the tip of South America. But their population is now limited to the north and central parts of South America. These big cats prefer to live in forest areas, though they have been spotted around dry woodland and grasslands.

Black Jaguars are often wrongly called black panthers or black leopards. But a good way to identify them is by their large head and stocky forelimbs

Great variety

The body of a jaguar often depends on its habitat. Those living in dense forested areas are smaller than the ones living in open areas. Forest dwellers are also darker in colour for better camouflage.

Females keep their cubs safe in caves, rocky dens or holes in the forest floor

■ Jaguars climb trees, though they are not as agile as leopards. These cats prefer to hunt monkeys in the lower branches of trees of the rainforest

FACT FILE
Length
1.5-2.5 m (5-8 feet)
Average weight
70-120 kg
(154-265 pounds)
Litter Size
1-4 cubs
Life Span
12-16 years
Size of cub
0.7-1 kg
(1.5-2 pounds)

In danger

There was a sharp fall in the jaguar population in the 1960s and 1970s. As many as 18,000 jaguars were killed every year for their coats. While jaguar fur is no longer in fashion, the big cat is still under threat. Many organisations are trying to protect the animal and the forests where they live.

INTERESTING FACT!

Jaguars are revered in many ancient cultures. The Mayans believed that Jaguar, the god of the underworld, helped the sun to travel under the Earth at night, making sure that it rose again the following morning.

Munching time

Even its hunting habits vary according to its habitat. If they live close to humans, jaguars hunt at night. Jaguars that live in the wild prefer to hunt during the day. They hunt cattle, horses, deer, reptiles, monkeys and even fish.

■ Jaguars like to live close to water. They are experts in catching fish and will often tackle turtles, dragging them out from the water and crushing their shells with their powerful jaws

59

Lynx and Ocelot

Not all big cats are as huge as lions, tigers or leopards. Lynx and ocelots are much smaller in size but that does not make them any less awesome. Both these animals are good hunters. But, like most big cats, they too are in danger of extinction.

■ Young ocelots are very tameable in their early years

Hungry lynx

Lynx live in parts of Africa, Asia, Europe, and North America. They prefer to stay in forests or in rocky, brush-covered places. They hunt mainly at night and feed on rabbits and other small animals. A hungry lynx can even kill fox and deer.

Spots and stripes

The lynx's fur grows long all over its body. The fur is light grey or greyish brown, long and silky. It is spotted and striped with a darker shade. Lynx have stubby tails and long tufts of hair on their pointed ears.

■ The lynx has huge feet with thick fur cover. These act as snowshoes and help it run swiftly over snow in winter. Lynx sleep in caves or hollow trees. They like to climb trees and lie on the branches

Dots galore

The ocelot's fur colour varies from reddish-yellow to smoky-pearl in colour. Its body is covered with black spots of different sizes. The spots on its legs and feet are like dots, while other body parts can have shell-shaped spots. The ocelot has a pink nose and large, translucent eyes.

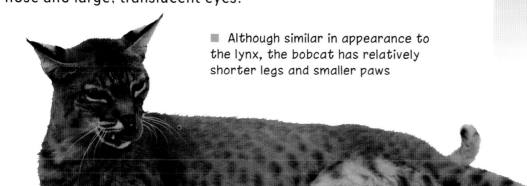

■ Although similar in appearance to the lynx, the bobcat has relatively shorter legs and smaller paws

Meal time

The ocelot is also known as the leopard cat or tiger cat of the U.S. The ocelot lives in an area ranging from Texas to northern Argentina. It eats mice, wood rats, rabbits, snakes, lizards, birds, young deer and monkeys.

■ Ocelots are widely hunted for their fur and their numbers have decreased sharply. There are now laws to stop the killing of ocelots

INTERESTING FACT!

The animal known as the African lynx is actually a caracal, which was thought to be a close relation of the lynx but has recently been shown to be a closer relation of the serval.

Pumas

A cat of many names, the puma is also known as the cougar, panther or mountain lion. It is found in Canada, North America and parts of South America. The puma has a small, broad head with small rounded ears. The cat's body is powerful, with long hind legs and a tail with a black tip.

■ Pumas have between one and five cubs at a time, generally two years apart. The average number is three

Coats of many colours

An adult puma may be either grey or reddish-yellow in colour. Its fur is fawn-grey tipped with reddish-brown or greyish colour. This animal has no spots, which is one of the main differences between a puma and a jaguar. They can also be solid black in colour.

Hunting skills

While on the hunt, the puma uses the strength of its powerful back legs to lunge at its prey with a single jump while it is still running. A puma can pounce over 12 m (40 feet).

■ A puma keeps under cover while stalking its prey. It then pounces, breaking its prey's neck or dragging it down to the ground

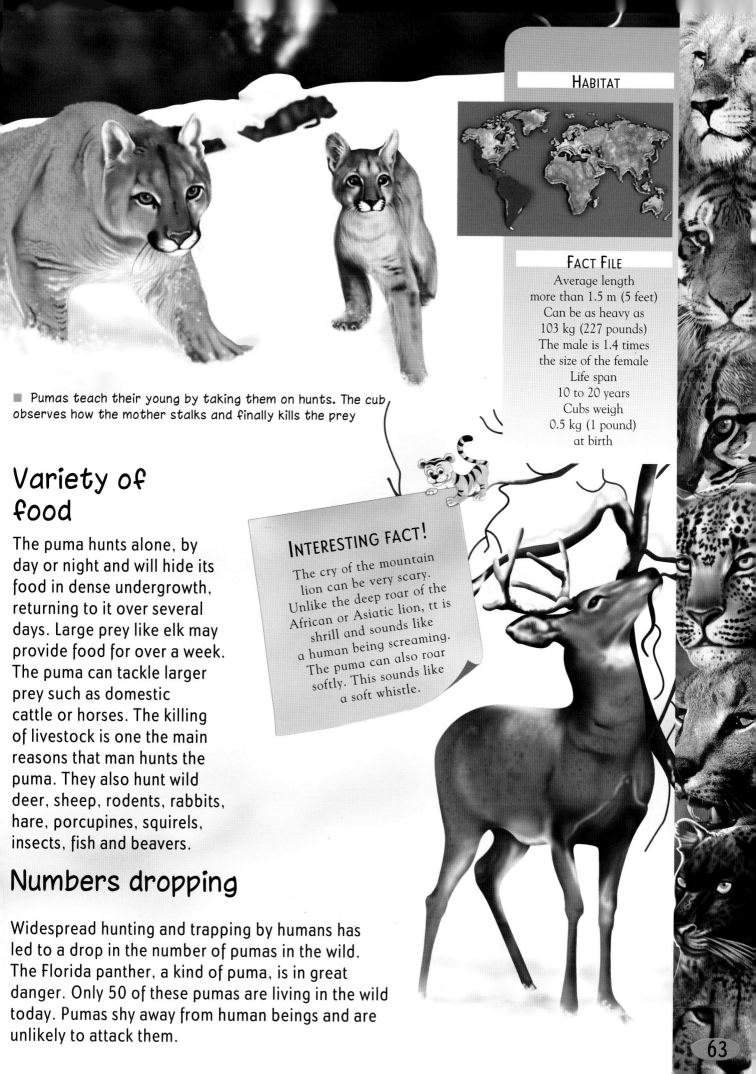

Pumas teach their young by taking them on hunts. The cub observes how the mother stalks and finally kills the prey

HABITAT

FACT FILE
Average length
more than 1.5 m (5 feet)
Can be as heavy as
103 kg (227 pounds)
The male is 1.4 times
the size of the female
Life span
10 to 20 years
Cubs weigh
0.5 kg (1 pound)
at birth

Variety of food

The puma hunts alone, by day or night and will hide its food in dense undergrowth, returning to it over several days. Large prey like elk may provide food for over a week. The puma can tackle larger prey such as domestic cattle or horses. The killing of livestock is one the main reasons that man hunts the puma. They also hunt wild deer, sheep, rodents, rabbits, hare, porcupines, squirels, insects, fish and beavers.

INTERESTING FACT!

The cry of the mountain lion can be very scary. Unlike the deep roar of the African or Asiatic lion, tt is shrill and sounds like a human being screaming. The puma can also roar softly. This sounds like a soft whistle.

Numbers dropping

Widespread hunting and trapping by humans has led to a drop in the number of pumas in the wild. The Florida panther, a kind of puma, is in great danger. Only 50 of these pumas are living in the wild today. Pumas shy away from human beings and are unlikely to attack them.

SHARKS

Dive into the deep blue sea and learn about the life of sharks!

A Shark's Tale

Sharks are amongst the most feared creatures on Earth, and only the very brave dare to go near them. They are meat lovers and have been around since before even the dinosaurs! Found in oceans, seas and rivers, they rule the waters with their sharp teeth and swift movements. Sharks are related to fish, yet they differ in many ways.

Bony matters

While most fish have skeletons made of bones, the shark skeleton is made up entirely of cartilage. Cartilage is the same flexible material that is found inside your ears and nose. It makes the shark lighter in weight and helps it to swim faster.

Living dens

Sharks can be found in most oceans and seas. Large and more active sharks usually stay near the surface or the middle of the ocean. The smaller ones prefer the ocean floor. Some sharks live near the coast and can even enter rivers and lakes that are linked to the sea.

Dorsal fin

Long pointed snout

Gill slits

Pectoral fin

Pelvic fin

Anal fin

Asymmetrical caudal fin

Size matters

Sharks come in all sizes and shapes. Some are tiny, and can easily fit into the palm of your hand. Others, such as the whale shark, can grow to a length of 18 m (59 feet) and can weigh over 18,000 kg (39,683 pounds) – almost twice as much as an elephant!

Skin that protects

Sharks have a special skin cover. Unlike the overlapping scales of fish, shark skin is covered with small, tooth-like scales. These are called denticles. These protect sharks and make the skin very hard and rough.

■ Cartilage is elastic in nature, making the shark skeleton flexible. This helps sharks to turn around quickly

Body Basics

Living in the water can be tough. To meet this challenge, sharks are equipped with special features. All sharks have strong jaws, a pair of fins and nostrils and a flexible skeleton. Sharks are great swimmers but, unlike fish, they cannot move backwards.

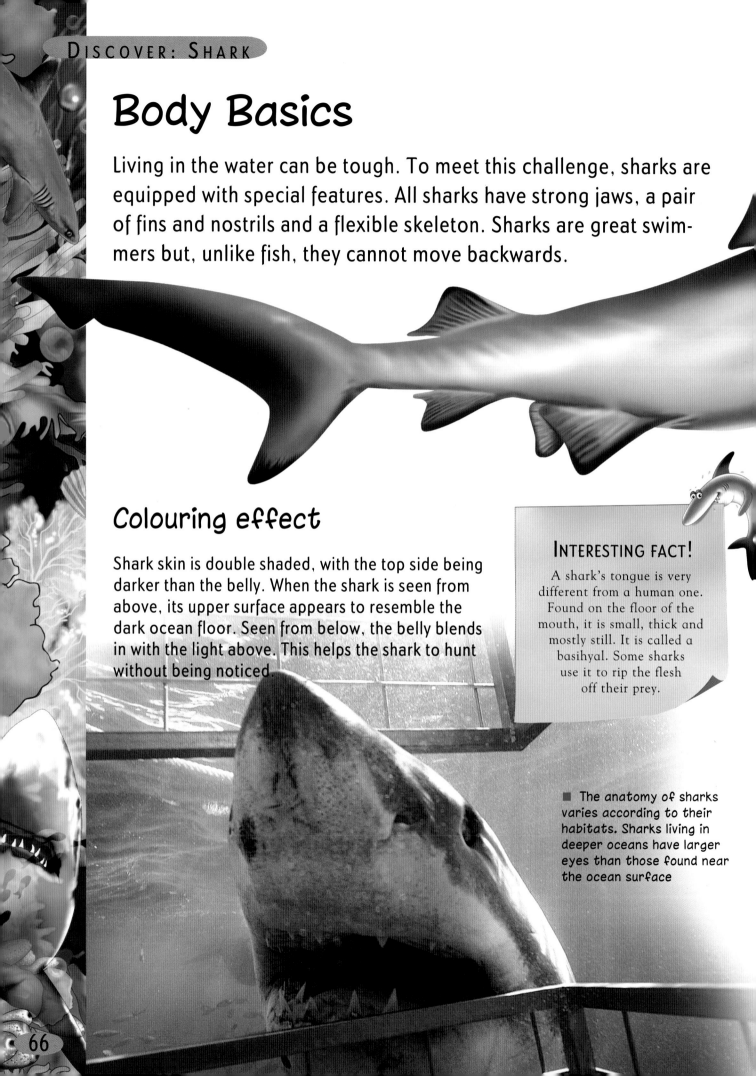

Colouring effect

Shark skin is double shaded, with the top side being darker than the belly. When the shark is seen from above, its upper surface appears to resemble the dark ocean floor. Seen from below, the belly blends in with the light above. This helps the shark to hunt without being noticed.

INTERESTING FACT!

A shark's tongue is very different from a human one. Found on the floor of the mouth, it is small, thick and mostly still. It is called a basihyal. Some sharks use it to rip the flesh off their prey.

■ The anatomy of sharks varies according to their habitats. Sharks living in deeper oceans have larger eyes than those found near the ocean surface

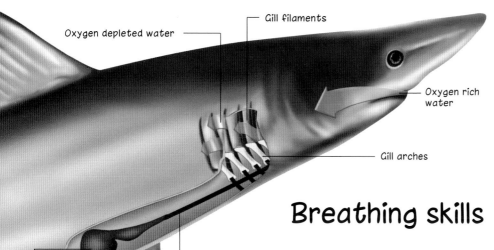

■ Unlike the gills of bony fish, shark gills do not have covers. Water must continue to flow across the gill slits for the shark to breathe

Gill filaments

Oxygen depleted water

Oxygen rich water

Gill arches

Heart

Ventral aorta

FACT FILE
Gill slits
Five to seven pairs
Skin thickness
Up to 10 cm (4 inches)
For health's sake
Liver oil is rich in Vitamin A
Uneven tails
The upper half is longer than the lower half
Matters of the heart
S-shaped and located in the head region

Breathing skills

Sharks, like fish, take oxygen from water. They have gill slits on either side of their heads. Water enters these slits and passes over the gill chambers, where oxygen is absorbed. Some sharks need to swim continuously to breathe, while others open and close their mouths to pump the water in.

■ Most sharks have five pairs of gills, while bony fish have just one. The broadnose sevengill shark, however, has seven pairs of gills

Oil Tank!

The largest organ in a shark is the liver, which is filled with oil. Since oil is lighter than water, it keeps the shark from sinking. Despite this, sharks must swim constantly to keep afloat. The liver also functions as a storehouse of energy.

■ Sharks usually have blunt snouts. But sawsharks have long snouts with toothed edges, which help them to dig out prey from the ocean floor or to slash at fish passing by

Torpedo-like!

Most sharks have a rounded body that tapers at both ends. This torpedo-like shape helps them while swimming. But some sharks, like the angelshark, have a flat body. This helps them to live at the bottom of the ocean.

■ The unique shape of the hammerhead shark's head helps it to get a better view of its surroundings

Shark Senses

Sharks have all the senses that humans do – and something extra too! Sharks can not only smell, see, feel, hear and taste. They also have a sixth sense. Their senses help them to hunt and travel great distances.

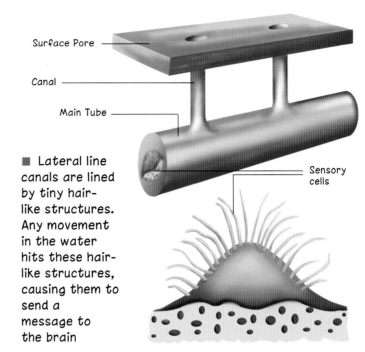

Surface Pore

Canal

Main Tube

Sensory cells

■ Lateral line canals are lined by tiny hair-like structures. Any movement in the water hits these hair-like structures, causing them to send a message to the brain

Line of action

Sharks have fluid-filled canals that run from head to toe on both sides of their body. This is called the lateral line. It enables the shark to sense movements in water. Some scientists believe that the lateral line can also detect low sounds.

Sixth sense

While electricity usually comes from wires and batteries, all living creatures also produce weak electric fields. Sharks are able to detect these with the help of their sixth sense. Tiny pores on the shark's snout lead to jelly-filled sacs known as the ampullae of Lorenzini that help them detect electrical fields.

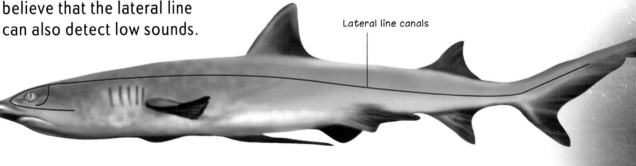

Lateral line canals

Smelly matters

In general, the nostrils of sharks are located on the underside of their snouts. They are used for smelling and not for breathing. Some sharks have nasal barbels, which look like thick whiskers sticking out from the bottom of the snout. Barbels help the shark to feel and taste.

■ Blind sharks cannot see. They hunt for their prey by using their nasal barbels

■ Certain sharks, such as the nurse shark, have openings called spiracles just behind their eyes. The shark uses these spiracles to breathe while hunting or feeding

Looking on

Sharks have very good eyesight, even better than ours. A shark's eye, like that of a cat, can contract or expand according to the light. This helps them to see in dim light. Sharks can also see colours.

INTERESTING FACT!

Sharks do not have external ear flaps. Instead, their ears are inside their heads, on both sides of the brain case. Each ear leads to a small pore on the shark's head.

■ The great white shark has a keen sense of smell. It can detect a drop of blood in 100 litres (176 pints) of water!

69

Toothy Terrors

A shark's only proper weapon is its mouth. The mouth is below the snout in all species except the angelshark, the megamouth, whale shark and wobbegong shark. These species have their mouths at the end of their snouts. The two most important parts of a shark's mouth are the teeth and the jaws.

Great white shark

Tearing and crushing

Sharks do not chew their food, but gulp it down whole. They use their teeth only to tear the food into mouth-sized pieces. Some sharks also crush the shell of their prey with their teeth.

Sand tiger

Mako

Big bite

In most animals, the lower jaw moves freely, but the upper jaw is attached to the skull. However, in sharks, the upper jaw rests below the skull. It moves out when the shark attacks its prey. This allows the shark to push its entire mouth forward to grab its victim. As the lower jaw teeth puncture and hold the prey, the upper jaw teeth slice it.

■ Different types of shark teeth

■ The great white has large wedge-shaped teeth with jagged edges. The teeth of the Megalodon were three times larger than those of the great white

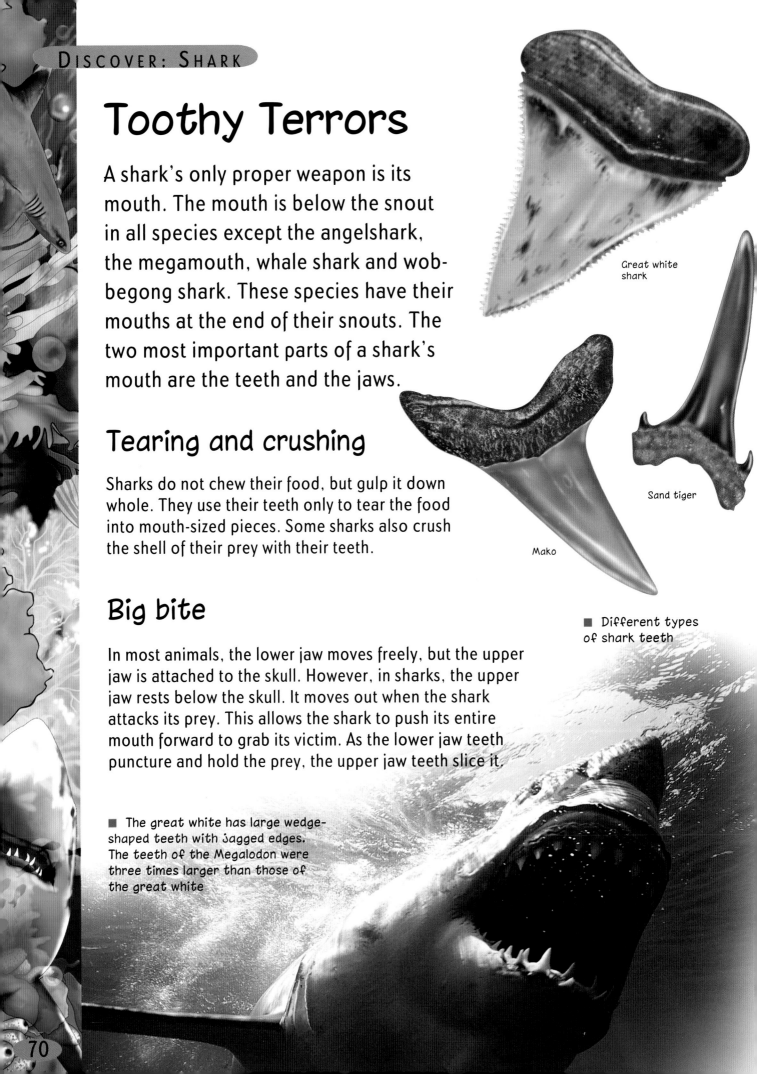

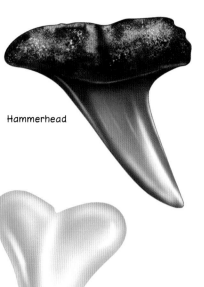

Hammerhead

Blue shark

Sharp new ones

Shark teeth fall out all the time. This is crucial, as worn out or broken teeth are continually replaced by new and sharper ones. The process takes place as often as every two weeks. In some sharks, like the great white, these teeth are arranged in several rows.

Tooth types

Sharks have a variety of teeth. Some have molar-like teeth, which help in the process of grinding. Others have razor-like cutting or pointed teeth.

■ Cookie-cutter sharks eat their prey by attaching themselves to it with special sucking lips. Once attached, they roll their body to cut out a chunk of flesh!

INTERESTING FACT!

The basking shark has very tiny teeth. It does not use them to feed. Instead, the shark swallows plankton-rich water. Special bristles inside its mouth, called gill rakers, filter this food as the water flows through them.

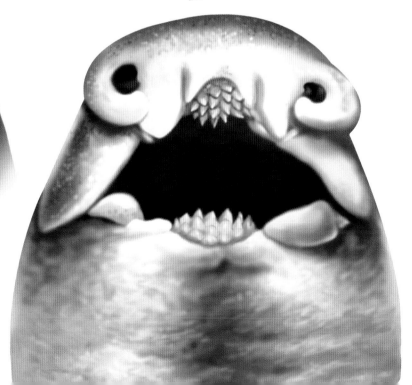

■ The Port Jackson shark does not have jagged teeth. Its front teeth are pointed for grasping its prey, while the back teeth are flat and molar-like for crushing

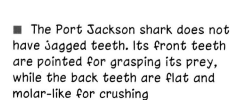

Young Ones

Baby sharks are called pups. A single litter could contain more than 100 pups! There are three different ways in which shark pups are born.

Laying eggs

Some sharks lay eggs like birds. The mother deposits the egg cases in the sea. The baby inside the egg gets its food from the yolk until the egg hatches. The parents do not protect the eggs. Horn sharks and swell sharks are egg-laying sharks. Such sharks are known as oviparous sharks.

Birth of a shark

Sharks like the hammerhead give birth to pups. The eggs hatch inside the mother's body and the babies get their food from the mother directly. Sharks that give birth to their young in this manner are called viviparous sharks. Lemon sharks, hammerheads, bull sharks and whale sharks are all types of viviparous sharks.

■ Horn shark eggs are spiral shaped and hatch six to nine months after being laid. The pups are usually 15-17 cm (5.9-6.7 inches) long

■ Certain shark's eggs are also called mermaid's purses because of their pouch-like appearance. The egg contains yolk that the baby feeds on

Hatching inside

In some sharks, although the eggs hatch inside the mother, the young ones do not get nourishment directly from their mother. Instead, the babies feed off other unfertilised eggs. At times, they even eat up their brothers and sisters! This kind of reproduction is called ovoviviparity.

■ A shark giving birth. The newborn pup lies on the ocean floor for a while after it's born. It then pulls against the cord that links it to its mother. Once the cord breaks, the young one swims away

INTERESTING FACT!

Shark eggs are enclosed in a tough leathery membrane. They can be of various shapes – pouch-like or shaped like a screw. Some even have tendrils that attach themselves to seaweeds and rocks on the ocean floor.

Caring for babies

Sharks do not care for their babies. The young sharks are well-equipped to look after themselves. In fact, they swim away from their mothers as soon as they are born. Sometimes a mother can even eat her newborn pups.

■ The predators of young sharks include larger sharks and killer whales. Some small sharks are even eaten by huge fish like the giant grouper

Giants of the Deep

Huge sharks have dominated the oceans of the world for centuries. Although the largest sharks today do not compare in size to the Megalodon they can still grow to enormous sizes. Amongst the modern sharks, the largest are the whale shark and basking shark.

Not a whale!

Contrary to what its name suggests, the whale shark is not a whale. It is a shark that can grow to the length of a bus! The whale shark has a huge mouth that may measure up to 1m (4 feet).

Straining food

Whale sharks and basking sharks feed on plankton by straining the tiny marine plants and animals from the water. They swim with their mouth open and suck in water filled with plankton. The shark then filters its food through special bristles attached to the gills and swallows the food. The water is ejected through the gill slits.

INTERESTING FACT!

Both whale sharks and basking sharks are slow swimmers. They swim by moving their body from side to side. Neither of these sharks is a danger to humans.

Whale shark

Colourful skins

Whale sharks have light-grey skin with yellow dots and stripes. On the other hand, basking sharks are darker in colour. They are greyish-brown to black or bluish on the upper surface, while their belly is off-white in colour.

■ Whale sharks love fish eggs. They are known to wait for hours for fish to lay eggs so that they can eat them. They even return year after year to the same mating grounds where the fish release their eggs into the water

The big basking

The basking shark is the second-largest shark. It has a short and conical snout. Unlike whale sharks that travel alone, basking sharks often move around in schools of 100 members.

■ Basking sharks are so called because they cruise slowly along the ocean surface. This gives them the appearance of basking in the sun

75

Pygmies of the Deep

Not all sharks are huge monsters. Some are, in fact, so small that they can fit into your hand! The smallest sharks include the pygmy ribbontail catshark, dwarf lanternshark and the spined pygmy shark. But like their bigger siblings, small sharks have strong teeth, and a bite from them can be decidedly painful!

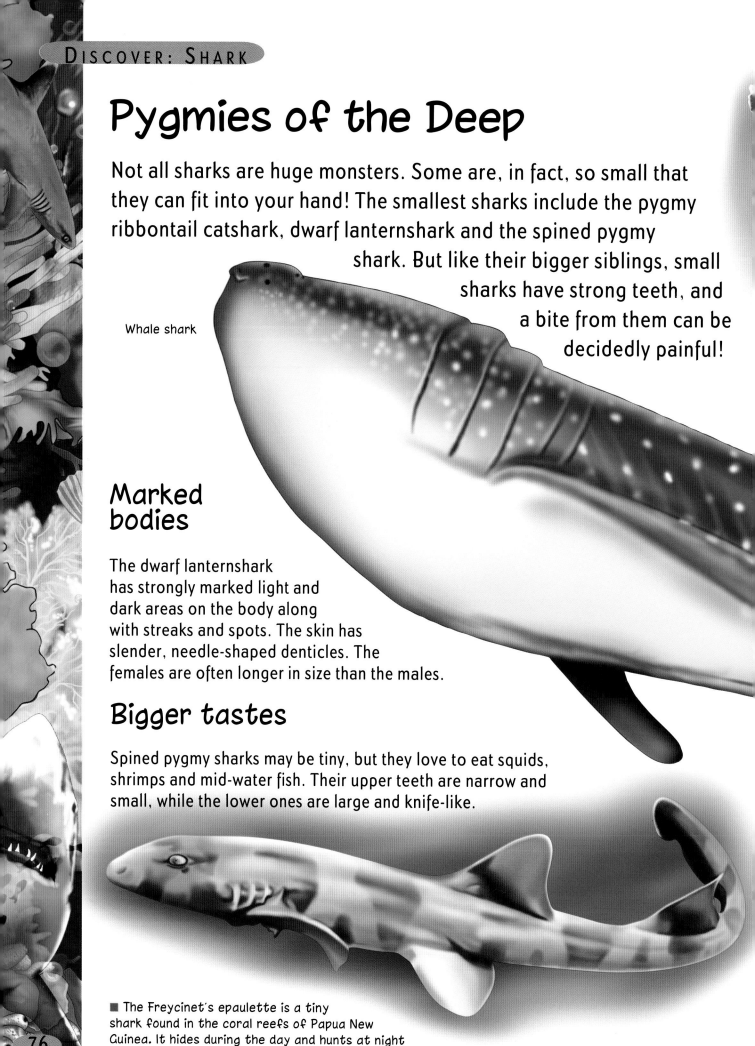

Whale shark

Marked bodies

The dwarf lanternshark has strongly marked light and dark areas on the body along with streaks and spots. The skin has slender, needle-shaped denticles. The females are often longer in size than the males.

Bigger tastes

Spined pygmy sharks may be tiny, but they love to eat squids, shrimps and mid-water fish. Their upper teeth are narrow and small, while the lower ones are large and knife-like.

■ The Freycinet's epaulette is a tiny shark found in the coral reefs of Papua New Guinea. It hides during the day and hunts at night

Tiny and glowing

Spined pygmy sharks are very sleek and have a bulb-like snout. They are dark grey to black in colour and have white-tipped fins. Their bellies actually glow in the dark. They live in deep waters and are rarely seen.

■ The pygmy ribbontail catshark lives on the muddy ocean floor, on slopes and outer shelves. It looks tiny compared to the huge whale shark

INTERESTING FACT!

Spined pygmy sharks are commonly found at the bottom of the ocean. However, these sharks are known to journey up to about 198 m (650 feet) at night to hunt in the mid-water zones.

Ribbons undersea

Pygmy ribbontail catsharks are dark brown in colour with blackish markings on the fins. They are found around Tanzania, India, Vietnam and the Philippines. The small shark feeds on small bony fish and crustaceans.

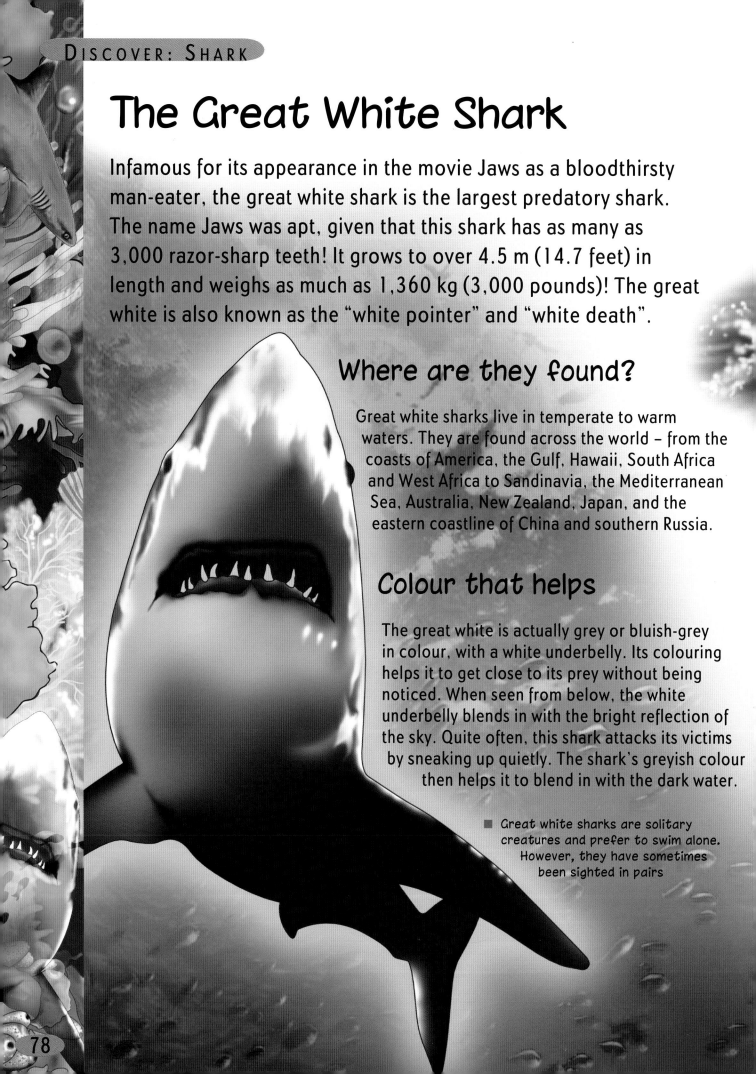

The Great White Shark

Infamous for its appearance in the movie Jaws as a bloodthirsty man-eater, the great white shark is the largest predatory shark. The name Jaws was apt, given that this shark has as many as 3,000 razor-sharp teeth! It grows to over 4.5 m (14.7 feet) in length and weighs as much as 1,360 kg (3,000 pounds)! The great white is also known as the "white pointer" and "white death".

Where are they found?

Great white sharks live in temperate to warm waters. They are found across the world – from the coasts of America, the Gulf, Hawaii, South Africa and West Africa to Sandinavia, the Mediterranean Sea, Australia, New Zealand, Japan, and the eastern coastline of China and southern Russia.

Colour that helps

The great white is actually grey or bluish-grey in colour, with a white underbelly. Its colouring helps it to get close to its prey without being noticed. When seen from below, the white underbelly blends in with the bright reflection of the sky. Quite often, this shark attacks its victims by sneaking up quietly. The shark's greyish colour then helps it to blend in with the dark water.

■ Great white sharks are solitary creatures and prefer to swim alone. However, they have sometimes been sighted in pairs

Fierce bite

With a mouth that is most often open, you cannot miss the rows of white, triangle-shaped, razor-sharp teeth. The shark's teeth can grow up to 7.5 cm (3 inches) long. Old or broken teeth are replaced by a row of new teeth.

HABITAT

FACT FILE

Average length
3.6-4.9 m (12-16 feet)
Can grow up to
6.8 m (22.3 feet)
Can be as heavy as
3,312 kg (7,302 pounds)
Number of babies
2-14 pups
Shark attack
30-50 attacks per year
Fatal attacks
10-15 deaths every year
Can swim as deep as
250 m (775 feet)

INTERESTING FACT!

Great white sharks are ovoviviparous. The eggs of the great white remain inside the body of the female shark until they hatch. The female then gives birth to live young ones.

■ Great white sharks often jump out of the water while chasing seals. This is called breaching

What do they eat?

Great whites eat dolphins, sea lions, seals, big bony fish and even penguins. Though they have earned a reputation for being man-eaters, they do not usually attack humans. These sharks are also scavengers, as they eat dead animals that float in water.

The great white first attacks its victim, injures it and then moves away. It approaches it later, when the pain and bleeding has weakened it. The shark does not chew its food, but rips the prey into mouth-sized pieces before swallowing them. After a good meal, the shark can do without another one for over a month!

■ Great whites are known to attack pelicans, but they prefer to eat seals

79

Tiger Sharks and Bull Sharks

Many sharks, like the tiger and bull sharks, are named after land animals. The tiger shark has dark stripes on its back, similar to the big cat. But as the shark grows older, the stripes often fade away. The bull shark gets its name from its flat, wide and short snout, which resembles that of a bull.

■ Tiger sharks have good eyesight, which is aided by a special gill slit called a spiracle. Located behind the eye, this slit provides oxygen directly to the eyes and the brain

Tough tigers

The tiger shark has a very large mouth with powerful jaws. The triangular teeth of these sharks have saw-like edges that can slice through many objects. The tiger shark is not a very fast swimmer and often hunts at night.

Junk eaters

Tiger sharks love food and will eat almost anything. Biologists have found alarm clocks, tin cans, deer antlers and even shoes in the stomach of dead tiger sharks! Tiger sharks also feed on other sharks, fish, turtles and crabs.

■ Tiger sharks often prey on albatross chicks, which fall into the ocean while learning to fly

Bull sharks

The bull shark lives near coastal areas. It is also commonly found in rivers and freshwater lakes. Bull sharks eat fish, other sharks, turtles, birds and dolphins. Interestingly, adult female bull sharks are longer in size than male bull sharks.

Danger zone

It is dangerous to go near bull and tiger sharks, as they are known to be man-eaters. Tiger sharks are the second-most threatening species to humans, after the great white. Bull sharks rank third in this respect.

INTERESTING FACT!

Bull sharks travel from the upper Amazon River to the sea every season. They cover a distance of 3,700 km (2,300 miles) during this journey.

■ Bull sharks hardly have any predators. But there have been reports of crocodiles eating bull sharks

The Swift Mako

Sharks are great swimmers, and the fastest among them is the mako. The mako's speed has been recorded at 31 mph (50 km/h). The mako is renowned for its ability to leap out of the water, to heights of up to 6 m (20 ft). They have even been known to jump into boats!

Shaped for speed

Makos are fast swimmers because of their sleek, spindle-like shape. They also have a long and conical snout. Their side fins are short and the tail fin is crescent-shaped to provide more power while swimming.

Other relatives

Makos belong to the order of mackerel sharks. Other sharks in this order include the great white, the porbeagle and the sand tiger shark. Sand tiger sharks are also called grey nurse sharks. They are found in most warm seas around the world. The porbeagle gets its name from its porpoise-like shape.

■ The sand tiger shark is known to swim to the surface and take huge gulps of air. It holds the air in its stomach to lie motionless in the water

FACT FILE

Can be as heavy as
450 kg (992 pounds)
Average length
2.7-3.7 m (9-12 feet)
Number of pups in a litter:
10-12
Size of pups
71 cm (28 inches)
Capable of swimming at
46 mph (74 km/h) in bursts

On the hook

Makos are a popular
sport fish. When hooked,
they jump around,
making them dangerous
to catch. Although makos
rarely attack humans,
they can be dangerous.

On the menu

Most makos live in warm waters. They feed on bluefish,
herring, mackerel and swordfish. Their teeth are long,
thin and sharp. This enables makos to catch slippery fish.
You can see their teeth even when their mouths are shut!

Dolphins

INTERESTING FACT!

Like most sharks, makos
are double shaded. Their
upper body is deep blue in
colour, while the sides and
the belly are white.
The blue shade helps the
mako to camouflage itself
while hunting.

■ Larger makos can
eat swordfish, marlins
and even dolphins

Ground Sharks

Ground sharks are the most common type of sharks. They have long snouts and a mouth that reaches behind the eyes. Their eyes are special too. Ground shark eyes have a lower eyelid that moves to cover the eyes during hunting. Ground sharks include hammerhead, carpet and swell sharks and all the requiem sharks, such as the tiger, blue, lemon, bull and certain reef sharks.

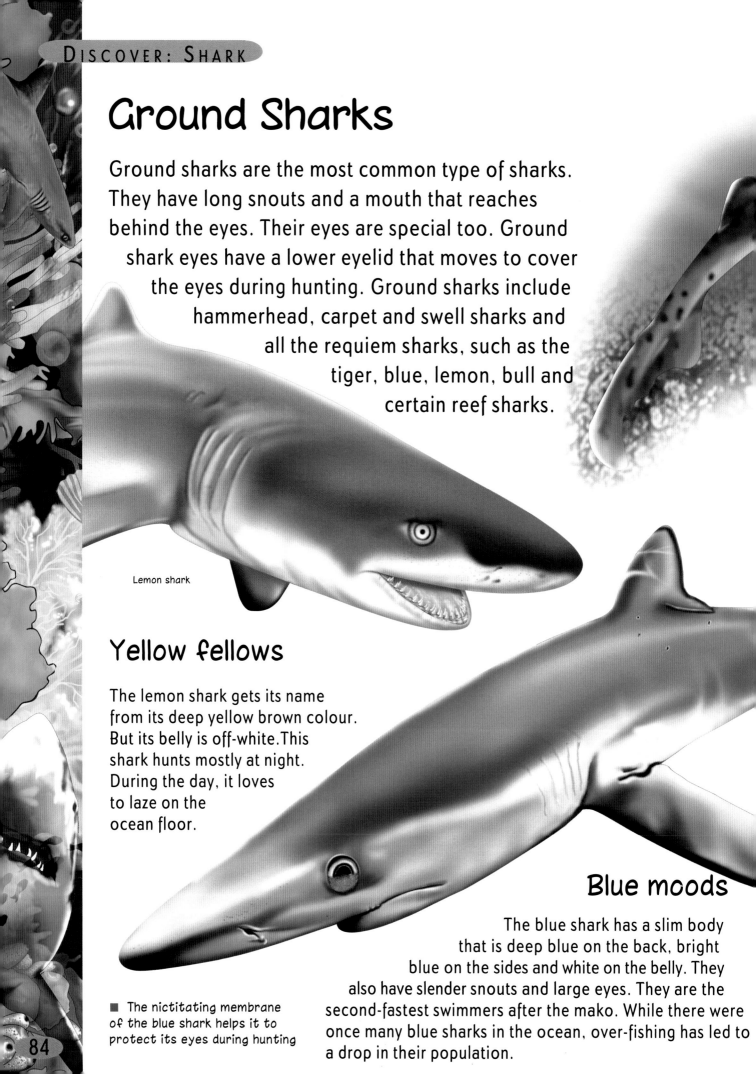

Lemon shark

Yellow fellows

The lemon shark gets its name from its deep yellow brown colour. But its belly is off-white. This shark hunts mostly at night. During the day, it loves to laze on the ocean floor.

Blue moods

The blue shark has a slim body that is deep blue on the back, bright blue on the sides and white on the belly. They also have slender snouts and large eyes. They are the second-fastest swimmers after the mako. While there were once many blue sharks in the ocean, over-fishing has led to a drop in their population.

■ The nictitating membrane of the blue shark helps it to protect its eyes during hunting

■ The swell shark can increase the size of its body by swallowing large amounts of water. This scares away the shark's enemies

Danger factor

Lemon sharks live near the surface and are often seen at bays, docks and river mouths. Though they swim close to human areas, lemon sharks attack only if provoked. Meanwhile, blue sharks live far away from the shores,

INTERESTING FACT!

The blue shark migrates the longest distances. It travels 2,000-3,000 km (1,200-1,700 miles) in a seasonal journey from New York State in the US to Brazil.

■ While most sharks eat other sea animals, Californian sea lions love to feed on young blue sharks

No fuss about food

Blue sharks can eat anything, but they prefer squid and fish. On the other hand, the lemon shark likes to feed on crabs, rays, shrimps, sea birds and smaller sharks.

Reef Sharks

Sharks live in different zones and regions of the ocean. Some, such as blacktip, whitetip and Caribbean reef sharks, live near coral reefs. Divers and waders often come into contact with such sharks.

■ Whitetip reef sharks are viviparous. A single litter could contain between one and five pups. Each pup is around 61 cm (24 inches) long

White cousins

The whitetip reef shark is grey in colour, with white tips on its dorsal fin and tail. It is slender and has a broad head. It feeds mainly on bony fish, octopuses, lobsters and crabs.

■ The whitetip reef shark is often confused with the silvertip shark. However, the silvertip is much heavier, and its fin is lined with white, rather than tipped, as it is in the whitetip

Sleepy sharks

Caribbean reef sharks live near the coral reefs of the Caribbean. These sharks often appear to be asleep, as they lie motionless at the bottom of the ocean. They love to feed on bony fish.

The blacktip

The blacktip reef shark is very interesting to look at. Its body is grey in colour, but the tips of its fins are black. The shark also has a white streak on its side. The blacktip reef shark thrives in aquariums.

INTERESTING FACT!

Whitetip reef sharks are most active at night, when they roam the reef in search of food. During the day, the shark rests in coral caves. Whitetips rest in groups, but they hunt alone.

■ Unlike other sharks, the silky shark has smooth skin. This is because the teeth-like scales are closely packed. Although silky sharks are largely found in deep oceans, they also frequent deepwater reefs

Living zones

Reef sharks live in different areas and depths of the ocean. The blacktip reef shark is found on sand flats at depths of 15 m (49.2 feet). The whitetip prefers to live in corners and caves around coral reefs.

Angelsharks

Angelsharks have flat bodies, which make them look very much like rays. They often bury themselves in sand or mud, leaving just their eyes and the tops of their bodies protruding.

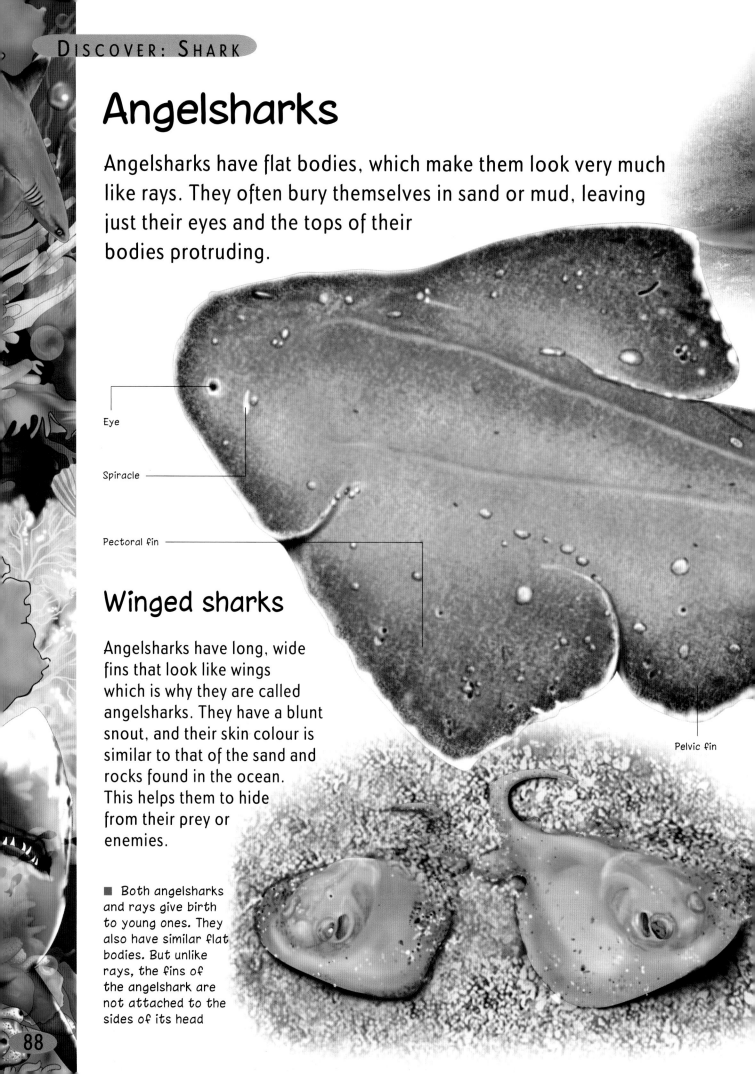

Eye

Spiracle

Pectoral fin

Pelvic fin

Winged sharks

Angelsharks have long, wide fins that look like wings which is why they are called angelsharks. They have a blunt snout, and their skin colour is similar to that of the sand and rocks found in the ocean. This helps them to hide from their prey or enemies.

■ Both angelsharks and rays give birth to young ones. They also have similar flat bodies. But unlike rays, the fins of the angelshark are not attached to the sides of its head

FACT FILE
Can grow up to
2 m (6.5 feet)
Number of babies
8-13 pups
Found at depths of up to
1,300 m (4,300 feet)
Can be as heavy as
27 kg (60 pounds)
Pups born at depths of
18.3-27.4 m (60-90 feet)

Hunting by surprise

The angelshark hides in the sand and rocks, waiting for its prey. As a fish swims by, the shark pounces on it suddenly. The angelshark eats fish, crustaceans and molluscs. It has small and sharp teeth.

First dorsal fin

Second dorsal fin

Caudal fin

INTERESTING FACT!
Angelsharks are not really dangerous if left in peace. But they can bite if you step on them. That's why they are sometimes called sand devils!

Bottom dwellers

Angelsharks live at the bottom of the ocean and prefer warm waters. They are mostly found in the Pacific and Atlantic Oceans. Angelsharks are not fast swimmers, but their prey is often even slower!

■ The angelshark feeds on a variety of reef fish including croakers, groupers and flatfish

Hammerheads

Hammerhead sharks are unique creatures, and can be easily spotted, even from a distance. They have a flat and rectangular head, which resembles a hammer. There are many types of hammerhead sharks. They can be differentiated by the shape of their heads.

Heady features

The eyes of the hammerhead shark are placed at the ends of its distinct head. The eyes can be as far apart as 1 m (3.3 feet), allowing the shark to view a larger area. Its flat head also helps the shark to keep its balance, as its side fins are very short.

Hammerhead Eye

Little differences

The great hammerhead has a straight head with a slight notch in the centre. The scalloped hammerhead has rounded corners on its head, while the smooth hammerhead has a broad and flat head without a notch. The bonnethead is smaller, with a shovel-shaped head.

■ The upper side of the hammerhead is dark brown, light grey or even olive in colour, while its belly is white

■ The great hammerhead migrates seasonally, moving to cooler waters during the summer

FACT FILE

Can grow up to
6.1 m (20 feet)
Can be as heavy as
230 kg (507 pounds)
Can live up to
20-30 years
Found at depths of
300 m (984 feet)
Number of babies
6-42 pups per litter
Attacks on humans
Around 35 attacks per year
Fatal attacks
Rare

INTERESTING FACT!

Angelfish act as official cleaners to hammerhead sharks. They pick up parasites from the sharks' skin and even inside their mouths. Interestingly, the hammerhead does not eat these cleaners!

Home sweet home

Hammerheads can be found across many areas. They can live at depths of 300 m (984 feet) and can also be found in shallow coastal areas, including lagoons. They are usually found in the Mediterranean Sea and the Atlantic, Pacific and Indian Oceans.

Stingray

Meal time

Hammerhead sharks eat crabs and fish. But their favourite food is stingray. The shark pins the stingray down using its "hammer". It feeds after sundown and hunts along the seafloor as well as near the surface. Large hammerheads also eat smaller ones.

Sharks with a Difference

The world under the ocean is a curious place. It is home to many living creatures of all shapes, colours and sizes. Sharks, too, belong to this wonderful world. Ornate wobbegongs, carpet sharks and horn sharks are just some of the odd members of the shark family.

■ The horn shark is not considered to be dangerous to people, but the spines can hurt if the shark is handled

The horned pig

The horn shark has a short and blunt head, and looks very much like a pig! It is either grey or brown in colour, with dark spots covering its body. The shark's small teeth are located in the front of its jaw, with large crushing molars along the sides. It is most active at night and feeds on sea urchins, crabs, worms and anemones.

The ornate ocean creature

The ornate wobbegong lives in the Australian and Pacific coastal reefs. It is called ornate because its skin has patterns in brown, yellow and grey colours. This helps the shark to blend into its surroundings.

Baiting for food

The wobbegong has worm-like projections around its mouth. The shark uses these to suck its prey into the mouth. Like the angelshark, the wobbegong also surprises its victims by camouflaging itself at the bottom of the ocean.

■ This varied carpet shark is a relative of the whale shark. But there are very few similarities between the two. The varied carpet shark is small and has a distinctive black `collar` with white spots

INTERESTING FACT!

The horn shark's egg cases are curiously shaped in a spiral, like a screw. Each case contains one pup and takes from six to nine months to hatch.

The ornate wobbegong

Goblins in water

The goblin shark has an unusual snout, which is long, flat and pointed. The jaws point out when the shark eats, making it look very peculiar indeed! It has soft, pale and pinkish-grey skin.

■ Little is known about goblin sharks, but it is believed that they are slow swimmers

DINOSAURS

An adventure into the world of the dinosaurs!

Evolution Through Time

It is generally thought that earth was created by a 'big bang', about 4,600 million years ago. The history of earth is divided into lengths of time or eras. Each era is further divided into smaller time spans known as periods.

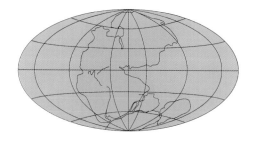

The land on the earth was one whole mass before it broke apart to form the various continents

The Tale of Eras

Eras and periods are based on the way rocks have formed and the fossils they contain. When scientists notice sudden changes in colours and types of rocks they mark these changes as the beginning of new eras or periods. The history of earth has been divided into four eras: the Precambrian period is the birth of earth up to the Cambrian explosion, when many forms of life developed; this is when the Paleozoic Era started. During this time organisms large enough to be see by the naked eye evolved; the middle period, or Mesozoic Era, is the era of reptiles, including the dinosaurs; the extinction of dinosaurs marked the end of this era and the beginning of recent life, or the Cenozoic Era. This era saw the rise of mammals including humans.

Many kinds of dinosaurs roamed the earth during the Mesozoic Era

Dino Facts

Originally the continents were joined together, forming one super continent known as Pangaea. The Jurassic period saw the division of Pangaea into Laurasia and Gondwana, which, in turn, facilitated the evolution of various species of dinosaurs.

The Origins of Dinosaurs

At first earth was rather hostile to life. Then, about 3,000 million years ago, microscopic organisms developed in the oceans. Simple life forms came to inhabit the sea. Gradually, these life forms evolved into creatures that could move on land and creatures that could fly.

Terrible Lizard

The name dinosaur means "terrible lizard" and it's thought that dinosaurs evolved from reptiles. Reptiles survived during the Mesozoic era because they fully adapted themselves to the changing environment. The first reptiles appeared around 300 million years ago. They evolved from amphibians. Unlike amphibians, which had to spend some time in water for laying their eggs, reptiles developed hard scaly skin that helped them live on land. Moreover, they laid hard-shelled eggs that hatched on land. Petrolacosaurus, Milleretta, Scutosaurus are among the earliest reptiles.

Ancestors of Dinosaurs

Scientists say that the now extinct Thecodonts, or Archosaurs, that lived about 230 million years ago, are ancestors of crocodilians, pterosaurs and dinosaurs as well. They were meat-eating quadrupeds with long jaws and a long tail. These creatures were socket-toothed, which means that their teeth were set in sockets in the jawbones. This made the teeth less likely to be torn loose during feeding. Thecodonts also had scaly skin. They closely resembled the crocodile, but they actually evolved into dinosaurs.

The Acanthostega was one of the first vertebrates to have recognisable limbs and be capable of coming on land

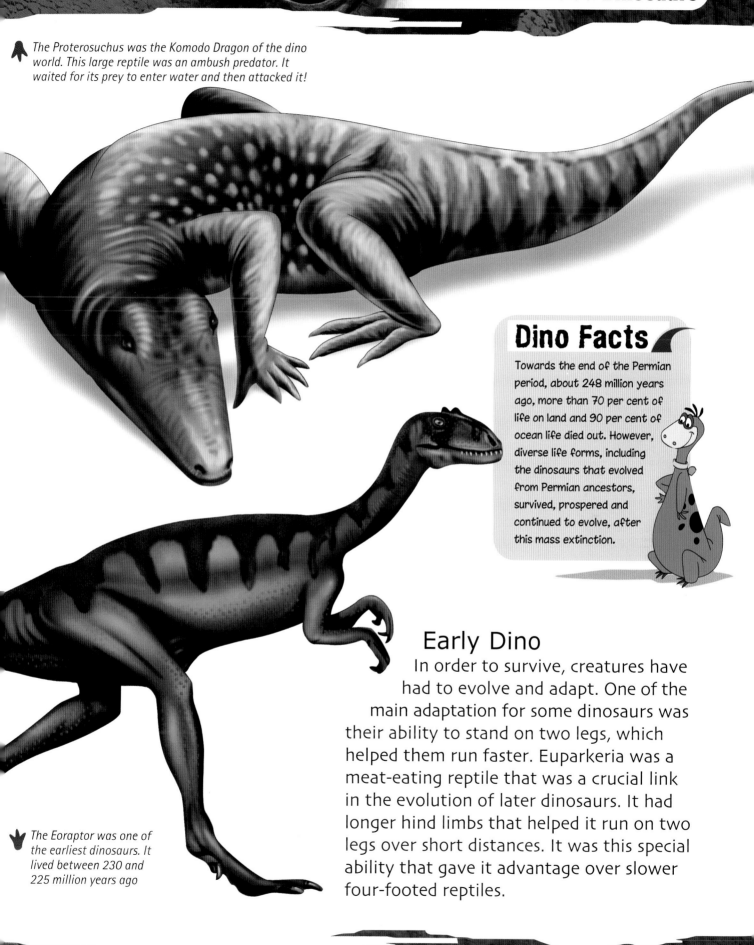

The Proterosuchus was the Komodo Dragon of the dino world. This large reptile was an ambush predator. It waited for its prey to enter water and then attacked it!

Dino Facts

Towards the end of the Permian period, about 248 million years ago, more than 70 per cent of life on land and 90 per cent of ocean life died out. However, diverse life forms, including the dinosaurs that evolved from Permian ancestors, survived, prospered and continued to evolve, after this mass extinction.

The Eoraptor was one of the earliest dinosaurs. It lived between 230 and 225 million years ago

Early Dino

In order to survive, creatures have had to evolve and adapt. One of the main adaptation for some dinosaurs was their ability to stand on two legs, which helped them run faster. Euparkeria was a meat-eating reptile that was a crucial link in the evolution of later dinosaurs. It had longer hind limbs that helped it run on two legs over short distances. It was this special ability that gave it advantage over slower four-footed reptiles.

Two of a Kind

Dinosaurs are classified according to the structure of their bones. There are two types of dinos — bird-hipped and reptile-hipped. Interestingly, it was the reptile-hipped dino that evolved into the birds we know today.

Bone Factor

Bird-hipped dinos are known as Ornithischians, and reptile-hipped dinos are called Saurischians. In Ornithischians, the pubis bone points downwards towards the tail, running parallel with the ischium. This feature is believed to have made the Ornithischians more stable while moving. In Saurischians, the pubis bone points downwards to the front.

Pubis

Ischium

Diagram of an Ornithischian hip, showing the pubis bone and ischium running parallel

Very Veggie

All Ornithischian dinosaurs were herbivores. They evolved in the Triassic period and died out with the other dinos at the end of the Cretaceous period. Many of them walked on four legs (quadrupedal). Stegosaurus and Triceratops are well-known bird-hipped dinos. Dryosaurus and Pachycephalosaurus are examples of Ornithischians that moved on two legs.

The Triceratops had three horns. One short horn projected above its parrot-like beak and two longer horns above its eyes

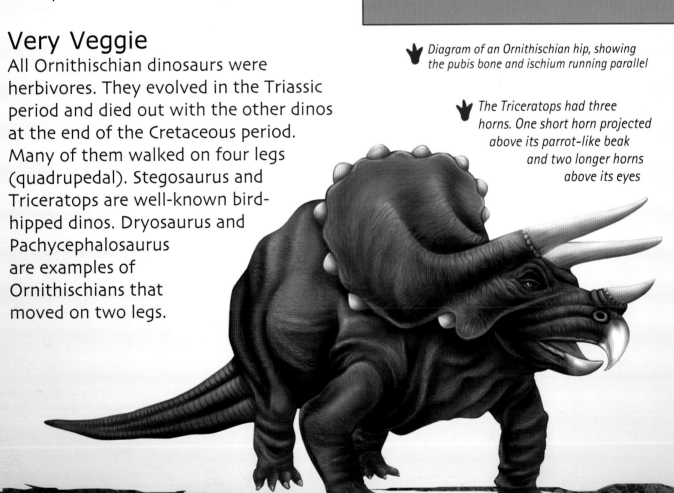

Two in a Group

There were two types of reptile-hipped dinos. One type ate meat and walked swiftly on their large and strong hind legs. The other type ate plants. These giants moved about on pillar-like legs. This means that ferocious predators like the T. rex, Velociraptor, and Allosaurus, as well as plant-eating giants like the Brachiosaurus and Titanosaurus, all belonged to the same group of Saurischian!

➤ The Vulcanodon was a bulky, long-necked and long-tailed dionosaur, about 6.5 m (20 ft) long. It had nail-like claws on its feet

◀ The Megalosaurus was a fierce predator about 9 m (30 ft) tall. It could kill even large sauropods

Dino Facts

In 1887, Harry Seeley categorised dinos into two types - namely bird-hipped and reptile-hipped. Nobody has ever questioned Seeley's classification. In fact, these divisions have proved very helpful in scientific research to this day.

Meat Eaters

Meat-eating dinosaurs appeared first about 225 million years ago and survived right until the time dinosaurs died out.

The fossil of the head of a meat-eating dinosaur shows its pointed teeth

Key Features

Most meat-eating dinosaurs walked on two legs. Their long legs ended in three toes with sharp claws. These dinosaurs had shorter arms, compact chests and longer tails. Their necks were curved and flexible. They were built for speed and agility that made them good hunters. Carnivorous dinosaurs had thin, blade-like teeth with serrated ridges. These ridges enabled them to cut and tear the flesh of the prey. But, believe it or not, some carnivores were toothless and had bony beaks instead! It is believed that they used their beaks to crack open eggs.

Killers or Scavengers?

Meat-eating dinosaurs were active hunters. They hunted in small groups as well as solo. Like tigers, they stalked their prey and attacked it when the opportunity came. Some meat-eating dinosaurs, however, were scavengers.

Small but fierce meat eaters ripped apart the flesh of dinos much bigger than them!

Small and Big

The first meat-eating dinosaurs were quite small — barely 3 feet long! Eoraptor, Coelophysis and Herrerasaurus were some of the small meat-eating dinosaurs of the early Triassic period. Dinosaurs gradually grew in size. Their limbs became more slender, their brains became larger and their eyesight became stronger. Larger meat-eating dinosaurs began to appear in the Jurassic period. Dinosaurs such as Dilophosaurus, Gigantosaurus, Megalosaurus and Ceratosaurus were large meat-eating creatures. At 12 m (40 ft) long, Allosaurus was the largest meat-eating dinosaur of the Cretaceous period.

Dino Facts

Meat-eating dinosaurs are collectively known as 'theropods' - meaning beast-footed. The famous American fossil hunter, Othniel Charles Marsh, is attributed with first making this classification in 1881.

◄ The Allosaurus had razor-sharp claws, about 15 cm (6 in) long, and razor-sharp teeth, about 10 cm (4 in) long

Terrible Carnivores

Meat-eating dinosaurs were fierce. Whether big or small they were top predators of their time. These skilful and clever hunters tore open the flesh of their prey with sharp claws and powerful jaws.

During a kill, the T. rex used its hind limbs to hold the animal down while ripping it with its teeth

The Tyrannical T. Rex!

The T. rex is perhaps the best known of all the dinosaurs. It appeared in the late Cretaceous period. About 12 m (40 ft) long, it was among the largest meat-eaters. The T. rex was a powerfully built dinosaurs that stood on two powerful legs. While hunting it could charge down prey at speeds of up to 36 km/h (23 mph). Its forward facing eyes are thought to have enabled it to see well. The T. rex had unusually short arms for its huge body, but these slender arms were equipped with two clawed fingers each that acted as hooks to hang on to the prey.

The T. rex is believed to have had the greatest bite force of any dinosaur!

Dino Size

The Deinonychus was barely 2 m (6.6 ft) in length but was a formidable predator nonetheless. It moved swiftly on two hind legs. Its most distinctive feature was the curved claw on the second toe of each foot. The claw was about 13 cm (5 in) long. During a hunt the Deinonychus would slash its prey with these claws. In fact the name Deinonychus means 'terrible claw'. These clever creatures hunted in packs and were able to wound an animal many times their own size.

The Deinonychus had a rather large brain: scientists believe that it was one of the smartest dinos

Dino Facts

Did you know that one carnivorous dinosaur preferred fish to meat? This was the Baronyx. About 10 m (33 ft) in length, this dinosaur had killer claws about 35 cm (14 in) long! It also had a narrow head and a snout like a crocodile. The spoon-shaped tip of its mouth helped it to scoop up fish from the water.

Other Carnivores

Many species of dinosaurs were part of the group that included all the meat-eaters. Dromaeosaurs, commonly known as raptors, and Orthinomimids, were two such species.

What's in a Name?

The name Dromaeosaur means 'running lizard'. Most of them were around 2 m (6.5 feet) long. These creatures were among the fiercest of all dinosaurs. The long, deadly claws on their feet and their big hands came in handy when they hunted in the jungle. Because they were small, most raptors hunted in packs. They were shrewd hunters. While on a hunt, they would look for the weakest prey.

This is the fossil of a Velociraptor's sickle shaped claw. The claw was about 9 cm (3.5 in) long

Many Kinds

Fossils have confirmed that there were many raptors in the Cretaceous period. The Velociraptor, Pyroraptor and Utahraptor are just a few of the Dromaeosaurs of the period. The Velociraptor was a fierce predator armed with sharp serrated teeth and a large sickle-shaped claw on the second toe of each foot. It used this claw to slash at its prey, wounding it until it gave up running away.

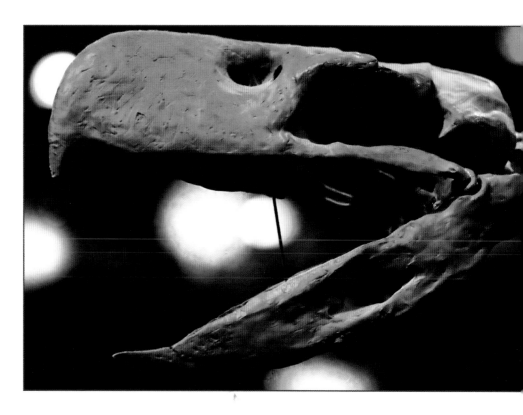

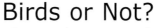 *Velociraptor means 'speedy feet'. It was a fast running bipedal dinosaur. This small dino was about 2 m (6 ft) long and 1 m (3 ft) tall*

The toothless Orthinomimids used their bony beaks to nibble on a diet of insects, small reptiles and mammals, as well as fruit, eggs, seeds and leaves

Birds or Not?

The Orthinomimids or 'bird mimics' looked similar to some of the flightless birds of today, such as the ostrich and emu. They had long legs, slender arms and toothless beaks. Their long, stiff tails enabled them to maintain balance when they ran. The Ornithomimus, Gallimimus, Deinocheirus and Struthiomimus are some well-known Orthinomimids of the Cretaceous period. Because these dinosaurs were toothless, they could not rely wholly on meat for survival.

Dino Facts

The Oviraptor was a bird-like dinosaur. It was probably covered with fluffy down and may have had feathers on some parts of its body. It also had a bony crest. Its arms may have been wing-like. It got its name, which means 'egg stealer', from a misconception that it stole Protoceratops's eggs. But, in truth, the Oviraptor was a doting parent.

Plant Eaters

Plant-eating dinosaurs appeared about 220 million years ago. They were much larger than the biggest meat-eaters. These giants thrived during the Jurassic period, which saw the growth of a variety of plants.

Pillars of Strength

Othniel Charles Marsh included these plant-eaters in a group named sauropods, or 'lizard feet'. Unlike its meat-eating relatives, this herbivore walked on all fours. It had thick, pillar-like legs, a long neck and a long tail. But it had a relatively small head.

The plant-eating dinosaurs were much more numerous and more diverse than the meat-eating ones

Food for All

These herbivores fed on ferns, mosses and leaves of tall trees. They used their teeth to pluck leaves from branches. The biggest ones, with long, flexible necks, could graze on the leaves of the tallest trees. The smaller ones fed on smaller plants and trees. These dinosaurs didn't need to compete for food as there was always plenty of food for all.

Fight Me if You Can!

Because these dinosaurs were heavy, they could not outrun their meat-eating relatives. But if they lacked speed, they had enormous strength. When attacked they lashed out with great power at their enemy. They used their tail as a whip or feet as giant crushers to inflict serious injuries on their attacker. Meat-eating dinosaurs usually stayed away from them.

➤ *Without plants there would have been no dinos. The herbivores ate plants and the carnivores fed on the smaller vegetarian dinos*

Dino Facts

The teeth of some plant-eating dinosaurs were not designed for chewing leaves, so they swallowed their food straight down. Many of them swallowed stones as well to aid digestion. These stones helped to crush the leaves in their stomach into a soft pulp.

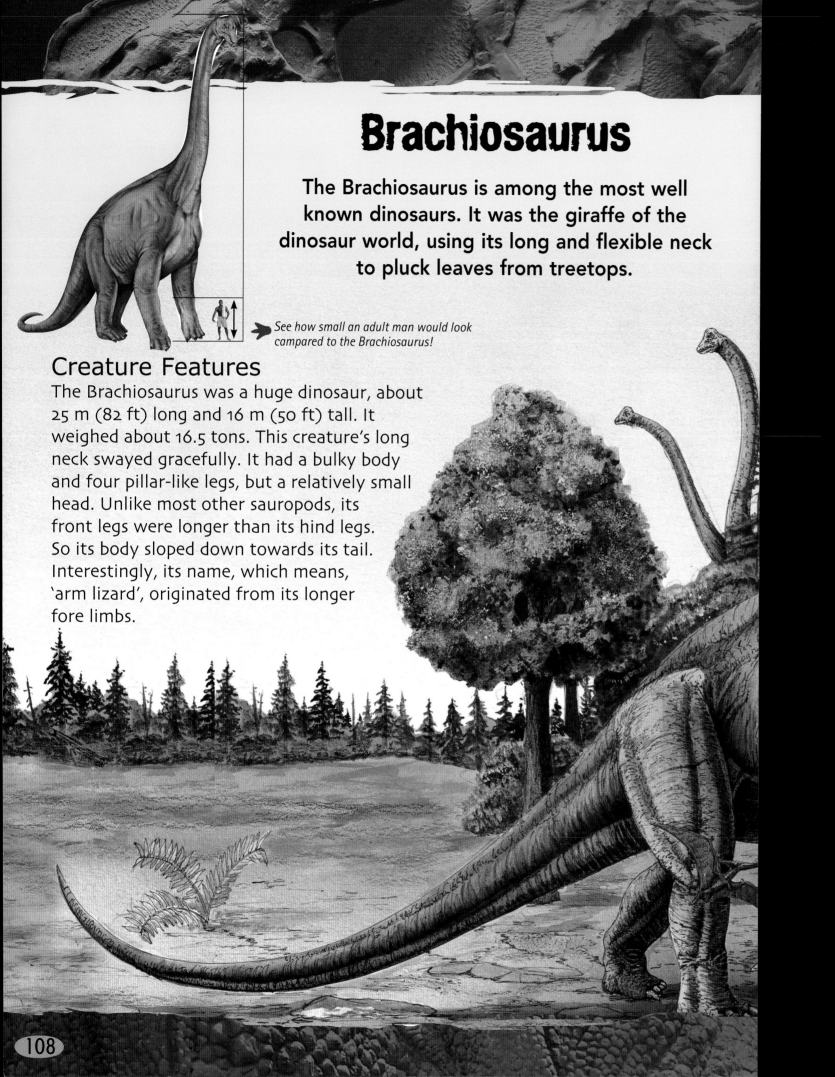

Brachiosaurus

The Brachiosaurus is among the most well known dinosaurs. It was the giraffe of the dinosaur world, using its long and flexible neck to pluck leaves from treetops.

See how small an adult man would look compared to the Brachiosaurus!

Creature Features

The Brachiosaurus was a huge dinosaur, about 25 m (82 ft) long and 16 m (50 ft) tall. It weighed about 16.5 tons. This creature's long neck swayed gracefully. It had a bulky body and four pillar-like legs, but a relatively small head. Unlike most other sauropods, its front legs were longer than its hind legs. So its body sloped down towards its tail. Interestingly, its name, which means, 'arm lizard', originated from its longer fore limbs.

Veggie Meal

Brachiosaurus usually moved around in large herds. They spent most of their time searching for food. These dinosaurs ate ginkgo tree leaves, conifer needles, palm fronds and low-growing vegetation. The incredibly long neck of this creature helped it graze on leaves that grew high up and also cover a large area of foliage without even having to move its feet. It had 52 chisel-like teeth with which it tugged and nipped at leaves. It swallowed its food whole, without chewing it.

It is believed that herds of Brachiosaurus migrated to regions with more food when they depleted their local food supply

Dino Facts

The Brachiosaurus had nostrils on top of it head! This must have given it quite a keen sense of smell. The Brachiosaurus could probably smell food and other animals even before seeing them!

Huge Herbivores

There were many species of plant-eating dinosaurs. These dinosaurs evolved during the Jurassic and Cretaceous periods.

One of the Longest

At about 27m (89 ft) long the Diplodocus was one of the longest dinosaurs. Like most plant-eaters, it had a long neck. The Diplodocus' tail was about 14m (46 ft) long - equal to about half the creature's length! When these dinosaurs moved, their neck and tail were more or less at the same level and they must have looked like walking suspension bridges! The name Diplodocus, which means 'double beam', owes its origin to this dinosaur's long and flexible tail that had an extra length of bone beneath the tailbones. When attacked, this creature lashed its tail to scare the attacker away.

High or Low?

Until recently many scientists believed that the Diplodocus, like the Brachiosaurus, raised its long neck to pluck leaves from the tops of tall trees. But recent studies of its fossils suggest that the Diplodocus could not raise its neck much above shoulder height. This means that, unlike most other plant eaters, this creature was incapable of reaching leaves on treetops. So the Diplodocus must have lived on a diet of ferns and low-growing plants. This meant that it did not have to compete with the Brachiosaurus for food, which is probably how both giants managed to survive.

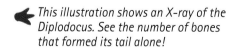
This illustration shows an X-ray of the Diplodocus. See the number of bones that formed its tail alone!

➡ *The Diplodocus was actually of a lighter build than other dinos its size: it weighed between 10 and 20 tons*

Dino Facts

Bones of the Titanosaurus were first discovered near the town of Jabalpur in India in 1871. They could not be matched with the bones of other dinosaurs found up until that point, so scientists concluded that they must belong to a new dinosaur. The new dinosaur was named Titanosaurus Indicus, or the `giant lizard from India`, in 1877 by Richard Lydekker.

Tapering Tail

The Titanosaurus appeared in the late Cretaceous period. It was about 20m (66 ft) long. Like the Diplodocus, it had a whip-like, tapering tail. When attacked, it used its tail as a weapon, flicking it wildly to scare the attacker away. If that didn't work, then it used its giant, strong legs to kick the attacker. Titanosaurus belonged to the group of Titanosaurs or 'gigantic lizards'. Some Titanosaurs were 30 m (100 ft) long! Titanosaurs had bony armour on their body and their skin was studded with small armoured plates for protection.

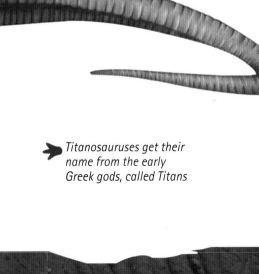

➡ *Titanosauruses get their name from the early Greek gods, called Titans*

Weapons and Armour

Over the ages dinosaurs developed many interesting features. In general, meat-eaters developed horns and talons to hunt, while plant-eaters developed armour to protect themselves from attack!

Armour-plated Dinosaurs

Nodosaurs were the first fully armoured dinosaurs. They appeared about 175 million years ago. Their name means "node lizards". They get their name from the many lumpy nodules of bones embedded in their skin. The other group of armoured dinosaurs were known as Ankylosaurs. The armour on Nodosaurs and Ankylosaurs comprised of flat or raised bony plates. The largest plates and spines were usually on the neck and smaller ones on the back and tail. Spaces between the plates were filled with bone pads so that the dinosaur would still be flexible enough to move.

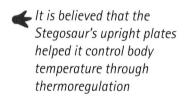

It is believed that the Stegosaur's upright plates helped it control body temperature through thermoregulation

The Euoplocephalus had a bony club at the tip of its tail to hit out with!

Scuted Dinosaurs

Plated dinosaurs include the Stegosaur family. These medium-to-large plant eaters had many upright bony plates, known as scutes, growing from their skin, on their backs and along their tails. These plates were arranged differently from Stegosaur to Stegosaur. Some had pairs of plates arranged along the spine to the tail, while others had plates running along the sides of their bodies. This armour was useful because it could be used for defence as well as attack. Scientists also believe that these plates were used in courtship displays.

Horned Dinosaurs

Also known as Ceratopsians, horned dinosaurs were widespread in the Cretaceous period. They ranged from the size of a turkey to the size of an elephant. While some dinosaurs of this group had horns on their heads, others had frills of bone around their necks – but all of them had a skull with a beak-like snout. Scientists believe that apart from helping in self-defence, the horns and frills were used to attract mates. During courtship battles the horned dinosaurs would lock their horns and push hard to decide the strongest.

The Triceratops would charge at predators much bigger than itself in self protection!

Dino Facts

The Scelidosaurus is thought to be an ancestor of the Stegosaurs. Its body was studded with many small body plates. Some of these were ridged, others cone shaped. Unlike the plates of the Stegosaurs, the plates of the Scelidosaurus were

Adapted to the Environment

There were many species of plated, armoured and horned dinosaurs. Each of them was uniquely adapted to its environment.

Stegosaurus

The Stegosaurus was the largest dinosaur of the plated Stegosaur family. About 9 m (30 ft) in length, this slow-moving herbivore was a long, low animal with a small head. Its hind legs were twice as long as its fore legs. It had 17 plates of varying sizes stretching all the way from its neck to the tail. No one knows for sure how the plates were arranged. They may have been in one straight row, in a staggered row or in two rows. This dinosaur also had two pairs of horn-covered spines at the end of its thick, stiff tail. When in danger of being attacked, the Stegosaurus probably flicked its tail in defence.

With plates and spikes on the body, horns on the head and club-like tail, the Ankylosaurus was fully protected from its predators!

Ankylosaurus

The Ankylosaurus was about 10 m (33 ft) long. It was one of the largest armoured dinosaurs. This dinosaur was a squat animal with a wide, barrel-shaped body. It had a wide skull and a short neck. Its fore legs were shorter than its hind legs. The height of this dinosaur allowed it to feed only on plants that were low to the ground. The whole of its topside was heavily covered with thick, oval plates embedded in its leathery skin. Only its underbelly was unplated.

Triceratops

The name Triceratops means 'three horned face'. Triceratops is the best-known horned dinosaur. This plant-eater was about 9 m (30 ft) long, and had a bulky body. It weighed about 9 tons. This dinosaur had a parrot-like beak, many chewing teeth and strong jaws. It used its small teeth to chew plants before swallowing them. It had a short tail and stout legs with hooved feet. This creature had a neck frill with bony bumps. It also had three horns. The two above its eyes were about 1 m (3 ft) long. But its nose horn was much shorter. When threatened, this dinosaur probably charged at its enemy with its horns.

The Stegosaurus had a toothless beak to nip at plants and small cheek-teeth to chew them

Dino Facts

It is believed that the plates of the Stegosaurus were covered with skin through which blood vessels ran. So, when this creature was threatened, extra blood was pumped through the vessels. This extra blood may have caused the plates to turn pink, sending out signals to other animals.

With its set of horns, the Triceratops resembled the rhinoceros

Bone-Headed Dinos

Over the years, a new type of dinosaur evolved. These dinosaurs were known as Pachycephalosaurs or 'thick-headed dinosaurs'. They got their name from their extremely thick skulls. They used their skulls to defend themselves from their enemies.

Head Bangers

The Stegoceras was about 2m (6.6 ft) long. It was a bone-headed dinosaur. A young Stegoceras had a relatively flat skull but as it grew, its bony dome became more and more prominent. The thickest part of the skull was 6cm (2.5 in) thick. This dinosaur had a strange bony ridge at the back of its skull. Male bone-headed dinosaurs head-butted one another when they fought for territories or mates. At times they even head-butted for fun!

Dino Facts

Stygimoloch was the only Pachycephalosaur with spikes on its head, which measured from 10-15cm (4-6 in) long. Its head also had many bumpy nodules.

See the Stegoceras ramming their thick skulls into each other to decide the strongest one in the group

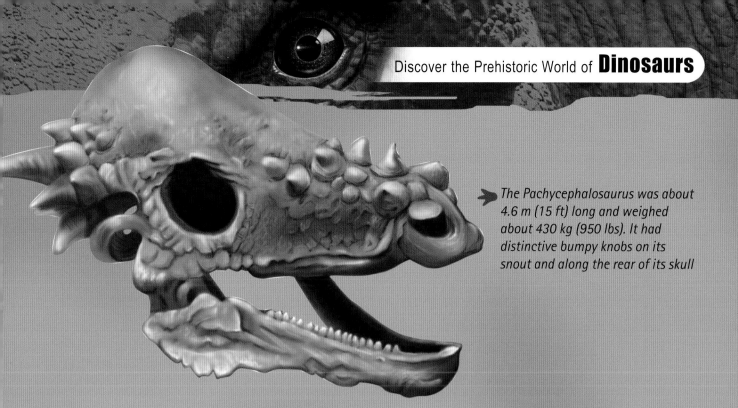

➤ *The Pachycephalosaurus was about 4.6 m (15 ft) long and weighed about 430 kg (950 lbs). It had distinctive bumpy knobs on its snout and along the rear of its skull*

Easy to Grasp

The Stegoceras moved about on two long legs. Its shorter arms had five fingers that helped it in grasping plants and pulling them towards its mouth. The claws on its fingers were used to dig up roots and other underground vegetation.

Biggest of Them all

The Pachycephalosaurus, a species of Pachycephalosaur, was one of the last bone-headed dinosaurs. The fossil of its skull proves that it had the largest skull of all bone-heads. Its skull was quite long — about 60 cm (2 ft)! And the bone that formed the dome was 25 cm (10 in) thick!

Of Teeth and Bill

During the Jurassic and Cretaceous periods a new category of dinosaurs evolved. These dinos, called Ornithopods, were the first plant-eaters to have true chewing teeth. They also had cheek pouches that helped them chew food better.

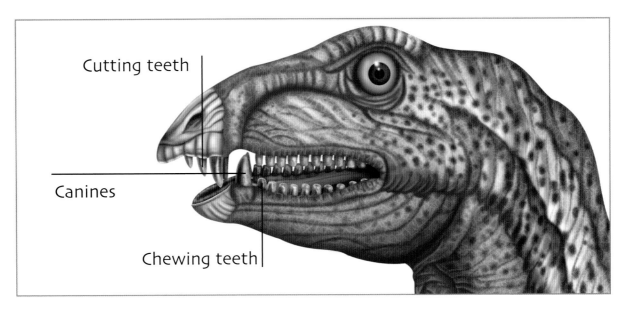

Cutting teeth

Canines

Chewing teeth

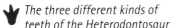 *The three different kinds of teeth of the Heterodontosaur*

Talk of Teeth

Ornithopods are divided into four different groups: the Heterodontosaur, the Hypsilophodont, the Iguanodont and the Hadrosaur. Heterodontosaurs had three kinds of teeth: cutting teeth, which were chisel-shaped; chewing teeth, which were ridged; and tusk-like canines. Only male Heterodontosaurs had tusks, which they probably used to spear prey and in courtship displays.

Teeth to Grind

Hypsilophodonts did not have any teeth at the front of their mouths so they bit off plants using their bony beaks. For chewing, they had ridged, chisel-shaped teeth. They chewed like today's cows and giraffes. Their jaws came together, with the upper jaw sliding outwards, moving in a circular motion. This helped to grind the food quickly and reduce it to a juicy pulp. Like Hypsilophodonts, Iguanodonts bit off plants with their bony beaks. Their small, molar-like teeth helped grind them into a pulp.

Dino Facts

The Maiasaura, the best-known Hadrosaur, was a caring parent. It made nests by scooping up soil. This dinosaur packed vegetation to provide a cushion for its eggs. It also covered its eggs with vegetation. When the plants rotted, they produced heat. This heat helped to incubate the eggs.

Duck-billed Dinos

Hadrosaurs had duck-like beaks which were broad and flat. These creatures also had about 1,600 teeth packed tightly into their jaws! Their teeth were arranged in groups of three across the jaw. This arrangement helped them crush and grind their food easily. They also had new teeth lined up below the jaw to replace the old ones that fell out.

The Iguanodon had a conical thumb spike on each hand about 5 to 15 cm (2-6 in) long. This may have been used for defence or in obtaining food

From Bone to Stone

Fossils are the preserved remains of animals, plants or other organisms. Dinosaur fossils have been preserved over millions of years. Even today, new discoveries are being made, constantly adding to our understanding of dinos.

Dino Facts

Would you believe that the skin, muscles, tendons and organs of dinosaurs have also been preserved as fossils? It is rare to find such fossils as soft tissue usually decomposes before fossilisation. Fossilised impressions of dinosaur skin are called dinosaur "mummies".

It is a rare and special find to discover the fossil of a complete dinosaur skeleton

Preserved in Stone

When a dinosaur died, it may have been quickly buried in mud or sand. Over many years, layers of more mud, sand and rock covered the remains. Due to the action of weather and minerals over a very long period of time, the bones decayed. The chemicals and minerals of the bones fused with the minerals of the sand and rock. This way the bones changed to hard stone, or fossils. Only the hardest parts of the dinosaur, such as bones, teeth, claws and horns, became fossilised. Studying them we learn a lot about those dinos. The conditions for a dinosaur to become a fossil are quite rare, so any find is an exciting event.

What Do Fossils Look Like?

A fossil has the same shape as the original object but it is actually a rock! So, a fossil is a rocky model of an ancient object. The colour, texture and weight of a fossil varies greatly from the original object. The colour and texture of the fossil depends on what minerals formed it. For example, the Kakuru dinosaur bone became fossilised in the beautiful opal stone!

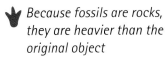

Because fossils are rocks, they are heavier than the original object

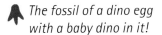

The fossil of a dino egg with a baby dino in it!

Types of Fossils

Fossils of dinosaurs generally fall into two categories — cast and mould fossils and trace fossils. In a mould fossil, a body part is buried by sediments that form a rock around it. When the body part decays, it leaves a hole or impression of the same shape. A cast fossil is formed when this depression is slowly filled with minerals leaving a stone of the shape of the body part. Trace fossils are records of the movement and behaviour of dinosaurs, such as their footprints and claw marks. These help us learn about their speed, the number of toes they had, etc.

The image shows the footprints of a dinosaur that have become preserved in stone over millions of years ago

Glossary

Adapt: To change to be able to live in a new situation

Ambush: Hiding and waiting to attack someone by surprise

Amphibians: Creatures that spend part of their lives in water and part on land

Archaeology: The scientific study of fossils and monuments of life and activities in ancient times

Barbel: Thin, whisker-like organs found near the mouth of certain fish and sharks.

Bask: To lie in warmth or soak up the sun.

Biologist: A scientist or an expert who studies living organisms.

Bipedal: Creatures that walk on two legs

Camouflage: The ability of some animals to remain hidden, usually because of their likeness to the surroundings, e.g. chameleon.

Continental drift: The gradual movement of the earth's continents

Carnivores: Animals that feed on other animals

Cartilage: A tough, elastic tissue found in the ears and nose

Cold-blooded: Unable to self-maintain body temperature

Constrict: To squeeze.

Crustaceans: Any of the creatures, such as crabs, lobsters and shrimps, which belong to the class Crustacea.

Ecosystems: Different beings living in one environment, depending on each other and working together

Endangered: Those species that are in danger of becoming extinct

Enzyme: A complex protein that speeds up chemical reactions.

Evolution: The gradual change in an organism to adapt itself to its environment.

Extinct: To die out

Felidae: The family to which all cats belong. The name feline comes from this word

Flexibility: Ability to bend without breaking.

Food chain: The system in where larger animals feed on weaker animals and organisms

Foliage: Plants.

Gall bladder: A muscular sac that is a part of the liver and stores bile.

Gills: The organ that fish use to breathe.

Habitat: Natural home of an animal or plant.

Hazard: Danger; risk.

Herbivores: Animals that feed on plants

Immune: Not affected by something.

Juvenile: Young one.

Keeled: Having a ridge or shaped like a ridge.

Mammals: Warm blooded animals, the females of which produce milk to feed her young

Marsupial: Those mammals where the mothers carry their young around in a pouch

Melanin: A black or dark brown pigment found in the hair, eyes and skin of animals and humans.

Membrane: A thin fibrous tissue that covers or lines cells and organs in animals and plants.

Mimic: To copy.

Mollusc: Invertebrates, such as snails, slugs, octopuses, squids, clams and mussels.

Nictitating membrane: A thin fold of skin under the eyelids that can be used to cover the eyes. It is usually found in reptiles, birds and certain mammals

Nocturnal: Of or relating to night; animals or birds that come out into the open at night.

Plankton: Tiny plants and animals that are found floating on the surface of seas and lakes

Predator: A carnivorous animal.

Prey: Animals that are hunted

Quadruped: Animals that walk on four feet

Radiate: To send out, or emit.

Reflex: Reaction; spontaneous response

Remora: A long, flat fish with spiny fins found in the ocean. It attaches itself to other fish and rocks underwater with the help of sucking discs on the top of its head.

Reptiles: Cold blooded animals

Retractable: Something that can be pulled back

Savannah: The grass-lands of Africa. In North America they are called the prairies and in South America they are called the pampas

Scavenger: An animal or bird that feeds on already dead or decaying matter.

Semi-arid: Place with low rainfall and little vegetation.

Skeleton: Body structure made up of bones of various shapes and sizes

Suffocate: To choke; to kill by not allowing to breathe.

Temperate: Moderate or mild in temperature. Not too cold or too hot.

Tendrils: Long thread-like structures.

Tissue: A group of cells in any living being

Torpedo: A cigar-shaped underwater missile that is usually launched from a submarine, aircraft or ship.

Vertebrates: Animals that have bones

Warm-blooded: Having a body temperature that does not change with that of the surroundings.

Index